D1135494

Haynes

Build your own
Computer

© Haynes Publishing 2003
Reprinted 2004 (three times)

Published by: Haynes Publishing
Sparkford, Yeovil, Somerset BA22 7JJ, UK
Tel: 01963 442030 Fax: 01963 440001
Int. tel: +44 1963 442030 Fax: +44 1963 440001
E-mail: sales@haynes.co.uk
Website: www.haynes.co.uk

British Library Cataloguing in Publication Data:
A catalogue record for this book is available from the British Library

ISBN 1 85960 973 2

Printed in Britain by J. H. Haynes & Co. Ltd., Sparkford

Haynes

Build your own
Computer

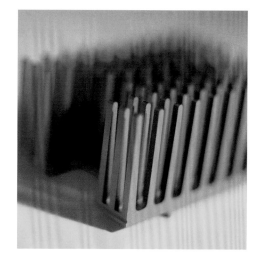

Contents

Introduction

You quite likely didn't build your own house, or your own car, or indeed your own television set – so why on earth would you want to build your own computer?

That's not entirely a rhetorical question, despite the subject of this book. We certainly don't want to turn you into a geek, and life is surely too short to fuss with unnecessary projects for the sake of it. But the odd thing is, the more you learn about how computers tick and what goes into their construction, the less inclined you are to buy one off the shelf.

It's not just that PCs are over-priced or over-complicated, although they are certainly both, but more that there's precious little to choose between a big brand name, a discount warehouse and someone selling anonymous hardware off a trestle table down at the local computer market. Computers are 95% generic. The same few companies make most of the kit used in most of the world's PCs. This kit is accessible to all. Given all of which, there surely comes a point where it must make sense to at least think about doing it yourself. How hard can it be?

Perfection inspection

Well, presumably you are ready to take the plunge. You'll be pleased to know that it's not hard at all. The surprising truth is that anyone can bolt together a computer, given the right parts, and we shall demonstrate this with our own Pentium 4 project later in the book. The trick, though, is getting the right parts, so to begin with we will concentrate on the key components.

Even if you decide not to build your own system, after reading this you will at least be in a very much better position to choose an off-the-shelf computer that suits your purposes. One glance at a PC superstore's displays will convince you that one computer does not fit all – and believe us, they don't carry all that stock with dozens of subtle permutations for the fun of it. But you don't have to compromise on the spec or be browbeaten into paying over the odds for a bog-standard system; you can custom-build your own computer from the motherboard to the mouse.

Our goal here is to help you build the 'perfect PC'. This, we suggest, fits the following criteria:

It must be suitable That is, it must be the right kind of computer for you. It's as simple as that, really. If you want to play games, you need powerful hardware in the multimedia department; but if you just want to plot your family tree and enjoy the benefits of e-mail, you really don't need wireless networking.

It must be flexible Your new computer should cover all the main bases from the outset. It must comfortably exceed the requirements of any software you care to throw at it and you should, for instance, be able to use a DVD encyclopaedia as easily as listen to an audio CD (or, indeed, make your own CD and DVD compilations). We'll help you work out what's important. But your habits will doubtless evolve over time and new software developments are forever expanding the horizon. Who knows what you'll do with your computer a year from now? Which is why …

It must be expandable The PC you build today, however basic or however fancy, must still meet your needs tomorrow. This requires some careful planning now and a strict adherence to industry standards. Come the day you wish to add to its features or boost its performance, an upgrade should be a pushover. True, you can never completely future-proof a PC but you can start with a solid base that will grow with you for years to come. Moreover …

It must be affordable Any mug can walk into a computer shop with upwards of £1,000 and emerge with a 'ready for anything' computer. But how many of its features, all of which you've paid for, will you actually use? Is all that 'free' software really a bargain? Would you perhaps have settled for a little less in the way of performance in favour of a larger monitor? The trick is scaling down or cutting back on the optional extras and concentrating instead on the core. Again, you – not the manufacturer's marketing department and not the store sales team – determine what kind of computer you really need … and how much you are prepared to pay for it.

If this all sounds like your kind of computer, read on.

PART

Planning the perfect PC

By doing all the donkey work yourself, you might justly assume that you can build a new computer for less than you'd pay in the shops. The truth may surprise you: you probably can't. But before you return this manual to the bookstore in a fit of pique, consider the reason why … and the reasons why it doesn't matter.

PART **1** # Four good reasons to build your own PC

While it's true that you can buy precisely the same components from a retail outlet as an OEM (see below) can source direct from the manufacturer, you pay a considerable premium. It's not a level playing field, with the result that it can cost rather more to build your own system than to buy an off-the-shelf identikit computer. And yet there are four good reasons why this really doesn't matter. These, indeed, are the reasons why we wrote this manual.

UNBEATABLE OFFER

Athlon *XP 5000+++ Processor!*
Massive *256MB DDR SD-RAM*
Super-Big *60GB Hard Disk (5,400rpm)*
Combo *52/ 48/12/6/2/1 x CD-R/RW/DVD+R/+RW*

2 x USB Ports + Modem!   *Integrated Audio!!!!*
15-inch TFT Monitor!!   *Six Speakers!!!!!*
Integrated Graphics!!!   *£££s free software!!!!!!*

CALL NOW 0800 24~~~~

Bargain of the century or a duff deal in disguise? If you've ever browsed the adverts and waded through specs, you'll know just how confusing buying a computer can be. So don't do it. Build one instead.

1 Satisfaction

Building your own computer is an immensely satisfying project. You're about to construct something from scratch that few people, even those who use them day in and day out, perhaps even you yourself, really understand. If that's not worth a pat on the back and a cup of kudos, we don't know what is.

2 Knowledge

To build a computer, you have to understand how everything fits together and be able sort out the important specs from the marketing hype. When an advert proudly proclaims 'Blazing Pentium 4 3GHz+ + + power!!!', and you can't believe the price, you can be sure that corners have been cut somewhere. But where, exactly? The answer is usually buried deep within the detailed specifications or hidden altogether: integrated graphics without an expansion slot for future upgrades, perhaps, or a cheap and nasty sound card, or insufficient memory. Read this manual in full and you'll know precisely where to look; build your own computer and you'll never be sold short again. The practical experience you'll gain in a DIY project of this nature is all you'll ever need to tackle computers with confidence for years to come.

3 Save money

Yes, despite what we said above, you can build a new PC on the cheap. The problem computer manufacturers and retailers alike face is one of having to be seen to offer the very latest kit at all times and at all cost – and that cost is borne by you, the consumer. But you don't necessarily need the latest kit, so why pay over the odds for PC performance that you'll never exploit? The key is compromising where you can and not where you shouldn't. By opting for a slightly slower processor and upping the ante elsewhere, you can make a PC that will outperform its shop-bought equivalent in every area – and save you money into the bargain.

4 It's the only PC you'll ever need

A bold claim indeed but one we feel confident in making. There are two really important points about building your own computer: you get to design it from the ground up to do precisely what you want it to do; and, provided you start from a sound base, you can expand, upgrade, re-equip and otherwise enhance your computer more or less forever. Flexibility is the key.

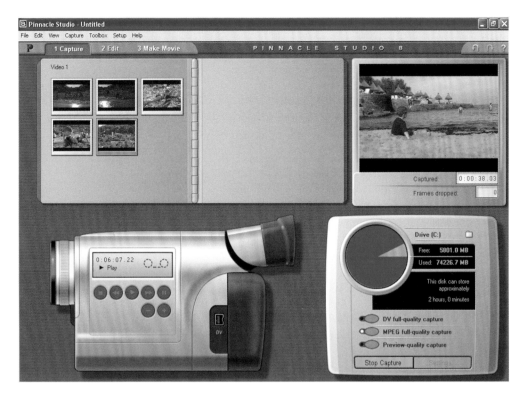

Pull the other one

But surely my computer will be out of date in a year anyway, you cry? Well, let's just examine that notion for a moment. Bits of it may no longer meet your changing needs, that is true. Let's say you acquire a camcorder a year from now and fancy editing your footage on your PC. You might even want to make your own DVD movies with the fruits of your labours. To do this, you'll need:

● a FireWire port with which to hook up the camcorder,

● a large hard disk drive,

● stacks of memory,

● a reasonably fast processor,

● and a recordable DVD drive.

To get started, you may have to add the FireWire interface, install a DVD drive, replace the hard disk and augment your memory (the existing processor will be quite fast enough so no change is needed there), but the point is you can do all this – and do it for a fraction of the cost of a new system.

Or let's imagine that a drive gives up the ghost somewhere down the line. No matter: a hardware failure is a temporary inconvenience, not a reason to replace your PC. Because you built the system in the first place, you'll know just how to fix it. Even if one day you have to replace the motherboard in order to acquire new interfaces, you can probably reuse the case, power supply, some expansion cards and drives, plus the keyboard, mouse, monitor and everything else. The notion that computers must be replaced every two or three years to keep pace with advancing technology may fuel the industry and keep the tills ringing, but it's largely a marketing myth. Are you really inclined to treat something that costs between £500 and £1,500 as a mere 'commodity', a disposable mod con with a useful life measured in months?

The downside?

Well … You will have to buy your operating system and application software separately instead of getting it bundled with a new system. This means extra expense. Then again, the software thrown in with new computers isn't really free; the cost is merely hidden within the system price, and you could end up paying unwittingly for several programs that you don't really want and would never dream of purchasing separately.

Nor do you get an all-encompassing service contract, warranty or technical support when you build your own PC. But would you rather do without your computer for a week or more while it's away getting repaired – or fix it yourself in an hour? Besides, every component you buy will come with its own full warranty.

New systems generally come with Windows and a few applications – some of them even useful – pre-installed. When you build your own PC, remember to factor in the cost of new software.

PART ① How to shop

Most PCs are constructed with components that are readily available on the open market. There's no great secret to it, really: all you need is a case, a power supply, a motherboard and a bunch of expansion cards and drives. True, some major-league manufacturers use proprietary parts that bind you to them for the lifetime of the computer – i.e. there's no other way to get spares and upgrades – but we're not concerned with such nonsense here.

An OEM would scoff at pretty packaging but there's a lot to be said for a retail product that gives you everything you need in the box. A motherboard, for instance, should include hard and floppy drive cables, a heatsink retention frame, installation screws, an I/O shield, chipset drivers, a manual and a warranty.

OEM vs. retail

An OEM, or Original Equipment Manufacturer, is a company that builds and sells computer systems with parts sourced from other companies. With access to the same parts, you can put together a system just as easily as any mass manufacturer. Indeed, should you wish to, you could put together the very same system. But better still, you can build the perfect PC for you: not necessarily the fastest computer on the block, nor necessarily the cheapest, but one that's custom-built to serve your needs both now and in the future.

There's really only one difference between components used by industry and sold to consumers, and that's in the packaging. Consumer products sport fancy boxes and fancier price tags and fill the shelves of superstores. You get everything you need in the box, including screws, cables, driver software and possibly an application or two. But an OEM has no need for frills and fripperies; rather, it buys bare components in bulk. A 'boxed' or 'retail' or 'consumer' (the terms mean the same thing in this context) Pentium or Athlon processor comes with a compatible heatsink and an instruction manual. The OEM buys exactly the same processor in trays of 1,000 with no extras whatsoever. Guess who pays less?

You, the intrepid system-builder, are not supposed to be able to get your hands on OEM stock, but it does filter its way through to specialist shops, direct vendors and computer fairs. So long as you're prepared to obtain your own cables, fittings, drivers and sundry other bits and bobs, an OEM component is usually a very good buy indeed.

When a power supply unit's air vents looks like this, you can be sure it has been round the block a few times. Nothing a blast of compressed air won't clear, of course, but you have to wonder how much life it has left.

New vs. old

You can buy computer components from many different sources. The first obvious distinction is between new and old, about which we need say little. A used expansion card, drive, power supply or even motherboard may well perform absolutely perfectly for years to come, or it may already be five minutes removed from hardware heaven. Truth is, it's usually impossible to tell just by looking. Buyer beware – big time.

By their very nature, used components are not cutting-edge. This is absolutely fine: you might, for instance, want to build a basic workstation for web surfing, e-mail, word processing and perhaps a little image editing and printing. Such a system requires only a relatively modest specification – even a Pentium II-based machine will be fine – and it would be wasteful and pointless to build-in surround sound and 3D graphics.

However, there are two important caveats. First, your computer will not be particularly amenable to future upgrades. Should it need a serious performance boost to keep pace with your changing habits, you won't be able to swap out the processor for a Pentium 4, or add an extra slice of fast DDR-RAM, or slot in a 8x-speed AGP card for gaming. You might not even be able to add a large hard disk drive, as older BIOS (Basic Input/Output System) programs don't always recognise or work with today's monoliths. Windows XP won't run on less than a 233MHz processor (and that's very optimistic indeed) so you'll likely be stuck with an older, less-adept operating system.

Now, all of this is fine so long as you know what you're getting into. Bottom line: today's bargain-basement project is unlikely to serve you well if you need a supercomputer tomorrow.

Also, and this might rather pain you, you can almost certainly pick up a complete, well-worn but perfectly serviceable second-hand computer system for much less than the cost of building one from scratch. Check the small ads, use an online auction site like eBay, try a reconditioned computer specialist like Morgan, or just ask around. Chances are you can pick one up for a song, perhaps sold without a monitor or extras like the keyboard and mouse. End result? A basic but functional and upgradeable-to-a-degree computer that's worth several times the price of its parts.

And so …

In short, when building rather than buying a computer, we believe it makes sense to adopt the very latest technology in several key interrelated areas, notably the motherboard, processor and memory. With up-to-date components at the heart of your system, a degree of future-proofing is guaranteed. Everything else, from the mouse to the monitor, from the scanner to the sound card, can be a compromise.

HP Vectra VEi8 P3-500 128mg Sony 17" Trinitron	£195.00	Buy It Now
DELL PIII-450 128MB 6.4GB CD SND **£104.00**	£104.00	Buy It Now
COMPAQ PIII-500 INTERNET READY +15" MONITOR	£135.00	Buy It Now
Pentium 3 Tower System DVD CDRW 17" & more	£200.00	14
Dell P-III 733 Bargain, 256MB, SFF, Dont Miss	£129.99	Buy It Now
HP Vectra VLi8 SFF System & 17" Sony T'tron	£104.00	18
P3 FULL Tower Server DVD CDRW 768Meg 19"	£170.10	15
MEGA VALUE PC, MONITOR, WINDOWS XP & FREE P&P	£399.00	Buy It Now

Older but still-functional computers are regularly replaced by individuals and industry alike. Shop around at an online auction site like eBay and you'll certainly find some bargains. Look out for pitfalls, though: an office-based machine may lack a sound card and speakers, and you should check whether the hard disk has been wiped clean of software.

PART

Where to shop

Several types of retailer are contenders for your component cash.

Computer superstores

Superstores cater more for people in the market for a ready-made computer or perhaps replacement drive or peripheral than the screwdriver-wielding DIY system-builder. Prices can be exceptionally good on certain lines – take advantage of special offers – but extras like printer cables can attract premium rates.

High Street independents

A mixed bunch, in our experience. Many smaller shops are staffed with clued-up enthusiasts happy to offer advice and help you with a purchase. Others are not.

Mail order/web vendors

Having lower overheads than 'real' shops, mail order and internet companies (often one and the same) should be able to offer better prices. They generally do just that, but remember to factor in delivery charges. Some also offer OEM goods, so check whether you're about to order a boxed, consumer-friendly retail product with a manual – or a drive-in-a-bag.

Dabs.com is one of the largest online high-tech retailers in the UK. Its extensive Dabsvalue range includes unbranded OEM-style products at rock-bottom prices.

Superstores like PC World offer a good selection of DIY components alongside complete computer systems. Check the Bargain Zones for the best deals.

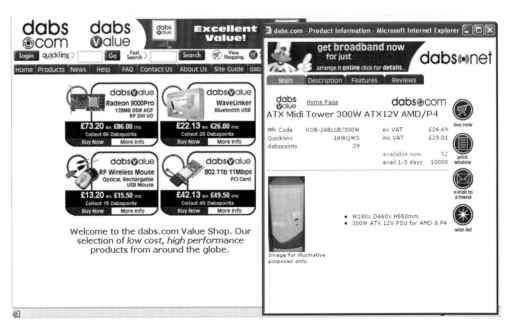

Snapping up bargains at a computer fair stall. See Appendix 3 for details of websites that list local markets.

Computer fair

Computer fairs are held regularly up and down the country. Here you will find the best prices of all, as long as you're prepared to haggle a little. However, the prospect of handing over a large wad of cash to a trader you fear you may never see again is rather daunting. Our advice is to leave your wallet at home the first time you visit your local fair. Get the feel of the place, note the traders' names and jot down some representative prices. You can compare these with shop prices later. By all means have a chat with a few traders and suss out who's prepared to offer free advice and a no-quibble return guarantee.

Official monthly fairs are policed by the organisers, and regular traders do tend to be trustworthy. You will certainly find OEM stock at a fair, and also salvaged components plucked from old PCs. If you need a stick of SD-RAM for an old motherboard, a fair is the good bet – as indeed it is for that old motherboard in the first place.

Golden rules include:

- Only deal with traders who openly display a landline telephone number (not just a mobile number) and address.

- Establish your right of return with the trader before paying, and check how you would go about making a return. Will you have to wait a month or more before you see the trader again?

- Keep all packaging and receipts.

B-grade stock

Damaged goods, items returned by customers without the original packaging, end-of-line components that have to make shelf room for newer stock, used systems sold off by companies upgrading their IT departments … all manner of functional but not-quite-perfect items qualify as 'B-grade'. The one constant factor is that this stuff is sold at a healthy discount.

You should get a guarantee of sorts with a B-grade item – perhaps 30 or 90 days – and (a matter of importance) any deficiencies should be clearly stated at the point of purchase. You have every right to get your money back if your purchase is dodgy in any way you weren't adequately forewarned about.

Take care, though. A monitor with a cracked screen isn't a terribly bright buy, nor is a fire-damaged power supply unit. But a sound card sold without a box, cables, drivers or manual might be a sensible cost-cutting investment.

And so…

Above all, shop around. Component prices vary wildly from place to place, often without rhyme or reason. Use a credit card wherever possible to take advantage of the added protection. Bone up on your consumer rights, too, just in case of problems. See Appendix 3 for contacts.

PART

Hard and soft options

In the next section, we'll look at the main components
that go together to make a computer. But first you must
decide what type of computer you wish to build.

Matching hardware to software

If there was a magic formula – 'to do X and Y buy Z' – we would
print it here. Sadly there isn't – but then you can't just walk into a
shop and buy the 'perfect PC' straight off the shelf. Nor can we
provide you with a definitive buying guide or make specific product
recommendations. For one thing, any such advice would be
instantly out of date; for another, one of the great secrets of
computer design is that it matters far, far less which brand name
you buy than whether a given component (a) adheres to industry
standards (no proprietary parts here, thank you very much) and (b)
has the right specification for its intended purpose. As a system-
builder, you have the opportunity – nay, the luxury – of being able
to make informed choices about every single part of your computer.

We will talk you through the hardware in Part 2. However, the
old adage of horses for courses holds true in the software stakes
too: the computer you build must be well-suited to its end use.

You don't need a room-sized mainframe to surf the web any more
than you need seven speakers to keep track of your household
finances, but you do need a good deal of processing power and a
swanky video card if you want to play computer games (plus a
joystick and a powerful sound card, and probably a set of
headphones to keep the neighbours sweet).

Spend some time now figuring out what you want to do with
your computer. In fact, make a list of all the software you know
or think you will buy, spend an hour in a superstore or browsing
a website, and make a note of all the system (hardware)
requirements. Then assume that these requirements are
understated by a factor of two – software developers are naturally
eager to appeal to the widest possible market – and make this
the basis for your hardware selection.

By way of illustration, here are a few typical applications:

Recommended system requirements

Application type	Typical example	Processor speed (MHz)	Memory (MB)	Hard disk space (MB)	Other requirements
Operating system	Windows XP Home Edition	300	128	1500	
Office applications	Microsoft Office 2003 Pro	233	256	790	
Image editor	Jasc Paint Shop Pro 8	1000	256	400	
DVD movie player	CyberLink PowerDVD 5	400	128	40	DVD drive
Digital video editor	Pinnacle Studio 8	1500	256	300	FireWire/USB port to capture video from a camcorder; lots of hard disk space for storing raw video; CD-RW, DVD-RW or DVD+RW drive to burn finished movies to disc
CD/DVD recorder	Roxio Easy CD & DVD Creator 6	1600	128	815	CD-RW, DVD-RW or DVD+RW drive
Business management	Sage Line 50 v.10	400	128	100	
Game	Commandos 3	2000	256	2000	3D video card with 128MB memory
Desktop publishing	CorelDRAW Graphics Suite 12	200	128	250	
Reference	Encyclopaedia Britannica 2004	350	256	275	Optionally, a DVD drive for the convenient single-disc DVD version
MIDI recording	Cubasis VST	450	256	300	MIDI interface; lots of hard disk space for storing recorded sounds
Antivirus	Norton AntiVirus 2004	300	128	85	
Utility suite	Norton SystemWorks 2004	300	128	150	

In all cases, we assume the presence of a monitor, mouse, keyboard, sound card, speakers, a CD drive with which to install the software and an internet connection

Check the specs

You can see at a glance that if you want to, say, edit digital video on your computer, you need a fast processor, lots of RAM and the means with which to connect a camcorder. Moreover, you'll need a further 13GB of hard disk space per hour of raw footage (or considerably less if your software lets you compress it on the fly). By contrast, you can burn an audio or data CD on pretty much any system at all so long as it has a recordable CD drive.

Perhaps the most noticeable thing about these figures is the importance of memory. Not one of our applications comes close to specifying a 3GHz processor – even the game will run satisfactorily on a 700MHz chip; remember, these are recommended rather than minimum requirements – and you're unlikely to be pushed for hard disk space with today's 100GB-plus drives. But memory is absolutely critical. Our suggestion, which we will reiterate later, is to compromise in almost every other area before skimping on the RAM.

Bear in mind too that multitasking on your computer eats into available memory and processor time. Just because you have 256MB of RAM doesn't mean you can successfully surf the web, edit digital video, construct a spreadsheet and play a computer game all at the same time.

Finally, remember that new versions of software titles almost always make heavier demands on hardware than their predecessors so it makes sense to start with a higher specification than you think you really need.

But we're getting ahead of ourselves. Let's turn now to the nuts

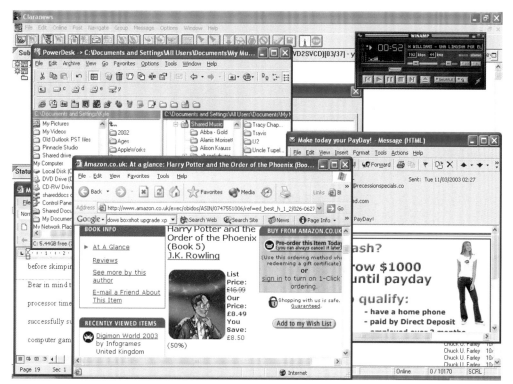

Trying to do too much with insufficient RAM can cause a computer to freeze. It's better to over-estimate your memory requirement from the outset than find yourself unable to run several applications simultaneously.

PART **2** # Choosing your hardware

Inevitably, this section gets rather technical, but as always we'll focus on what you really need to know and resist wallowing in the mire of jargon and the inner workings of microelectronics. You don't need to know that Intel's 4004 processor ran at a clock speed of 108KHz in 1971 to appreciate that today's Pentium 4 3.06GHz processor – some 28,000 times faster than the 4004 – is particularly well-suited to ultra-demanding software applications but definite overkill for the odd spreadsheet.

PART 2 Motherboard

The single most important piece of hardware that you will buy is the motherboard – the very heart of your system. The processor plugs into it, drives connect to it with cables, expansion cards live in special slots and everything else, from the mouse to the printer, is ultimately connected to and controlled by the motherboard. If you buy a PC from a shop, chances are you'll never think about or even see the motherboard; but when you build a system from scratch, it must be your primary consideration. Everything else follows from here.

QUICK Q&A

I'm considering a motherboard that claims to be 'legacy-free'. It sounds like a bonus but what does it mean?

It means it has no serial, parallel, mouse or keyboard ports and nowhere to connect a floppy disk drive! This might be a good thing but only if you already have, or intend to get, a USB mouse, keyboard, printer etc. and don't mind going without a floppy drive. It's certainly the way of the future. For this project, we couldn't quite bring ourselves to ditch these legacy interfaces just yet.

Integrated audio chip

PCI slots

USB sockets

Battery

Front panel sockets

BIOS

AGP slot

Input/output panel
(see p22 for details)

Integrated LAN chip

ATX12V socket

Heatsink retention fframe

Processor socket (socket 478)

Chipset (MCH)

Processor fan socket

Fan socket

Memory slots (DIMMS)

ATX power socket

Chipset (ICH)

Fan socket

IDE/ATA sockets

Floppy disk
drive socket

Form factor

This is a fancy way of describing a motherboard's size and shape, important because it involves industry-wide standards and ties in with the computer case and power supply. Form factors have evolved through the years, culminating since 1995 in a popular and flexible standard known as ATX (Advanced Technology Extended). There's not just one ATX standard, of course – there are MiniATX, MicroATX and FlexATX motherboards out there, all progressively slimmed-down versions of the full-size ATX. The upside of a smaller motherboard is that you can use a smaller case and reduce the overall dimensions of your computer; the downside is a corresponding reduction in expandability. A full-sized ATX motherboard can have up to seven expansion slots, while a MicroATX motherboard is limited to four.

Should you have a tape measure handy and wish to do some checking, here are the maximum ATX motherboard sizes as specified by Intel:

ATX	305mm	x	244mm
MiniATX	284mm	x	208mm
MicroATX	244mm	x	244mm
FlexATX	229mm	x	191mm

One technical benefit of ATX over the earlier BabyAT form factor from which it directly evolved is that full-length expansion cards can now be fitted in all slots; previously, the location of the processor and memory on the motherboard meant that some slots could only take stumpy (not a technical term) cards. Another is the use of a double-height input/output panel that lets motherboard manufacturers build in more integrated features. All in all, it's a definite improvement.

But from your point of view, the main attraction has to be the guarantee that any ATX motherboard, including the smaller versions, will fit inside any ATX computer case. That's the beauty of standards. Moreover, since the ATX form factor is now overwhelmingly dominant, our first cast-iron recommendation is

TECHIE CORNER

Chipset drivers You can't upgrade the chipset on an old motherboard but you can and should upgrade the chipset drivers. Technology inevitably advances beyond the native capabilities of any chipset, with the result that older motherboards can't always work with new devices (broadband USB modems being a particularly troublesome case in point). A driver update is sometimes sufficient to bring the chipset up to speed and hence make the difference between a useful motherboard and a waste of money. Driver updates can also improve chipset performance in key areas like integrated video. Pay occasional visits to the motherboard or chipset manufacturer's website and look for downloadable driver updates.

that you consider only ATX motherboards. Our second is that you go for a full-size ATX motherboard unless you truly have a pressing need for a small PC: the scaled-down, cheaper form factors are popular with PC manufacturers anxious to shave a few pounds from the price of a finished system but the true cost is passed on to the customer in the shape of reduced expansion possibilities. Don't limit yourself unnecessarily.

The most recent addition to the form factor parade is BTX (Balanced Technology Extended). This has a leaner, flatter form factor compared to ATX, and is specifically designed to facilitate adequate cooling in smaller computers. A BTX motherboard comes in three variations:

BTX	267mm	x	325mm
MicroBTX	267mm	x	264mm
PicoBTX	267mm	x	203mm

Some BTX motherboards also require new cases and power supplies. This is one to watch rather than buy right now.

A double-height input/output panel.

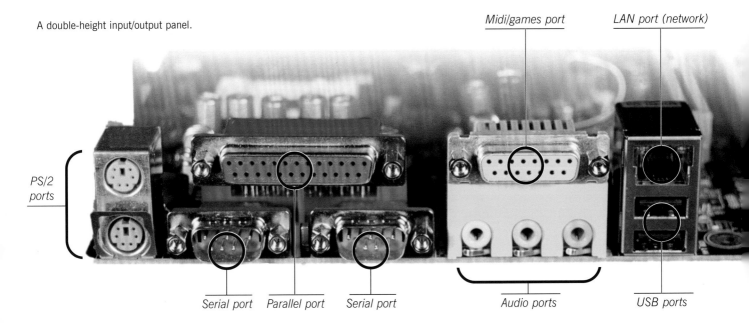

Midi/games port

LAN port (network)

PS/2 ports

Serial port *Parallel port* *Serial port* *Audio ports* *USB ports*

The chipset

The real meat of a motherboard resides in its chipset: a collection of microchips that together control all the major functions. Without a chipset, a motherboard would be lifeless; with a duff chipset, it may be inadequate for your needs. Indeed, as one motherboard manufacturer explained it to us, the chipset is the motherboard: don't ask what this or that motherboard can do – ask instead what chipset it uses, and there you'll find your answer.

So what does a chipset do, precisely? Well, at one level it controls the flow of data between motherboard components through a series of interfaces. Each interface, or channel, is called a bus. Important buses include:

FSB (Front-side Bus) The interface between the chipset and the processor.

Memory bus The interface between the chipset and RAM.

AGP bus (Accelerated graphics Port) The interface between the chipset and the video card. This is slated to be superseded by the new, hyper-fast PCI Express interface from mid-2004 onwards, but there's plenty of life left in AGP yet, particularly in the 8x-speed version.

PCI bus (Peripheral Components Interconnect) The interface between the chipset and the PCI expansion slots. As just noted, a newer interface called PCI Express should be available soon. This has a far greater bandwidth than even a souped-up AGP interface. Expect to find the first PCI Express slots appearing on motherboards in mid-2004 and thereafter finding widespread adoption as expansion card manufacturers gradually take advantage of the potential for increased performance. Just like AGP, various versions will be available, including 1x, 4x, 8x and 16x-speed.

ISA bus (Industry Standard Architecture) The interface between the chipset and the ISA expansion slots. This is now effectively obsolete.

IDE/ATA bus (Integrated Drive Electronics/Advanced Technology Attachment) The interface between the chipset and the hard drive/optical drives. As we note on p.45, a new improved interface called Serial ATA is now available. Opting for this now might be sensible future-proofing but the reality is that you won't see any benefits in terms of hard drive performance.

And then there are buses controlling the floppy disk, parallel, serial and USB ports, SCSI devices, built-in networking capability and any number of add-on features.

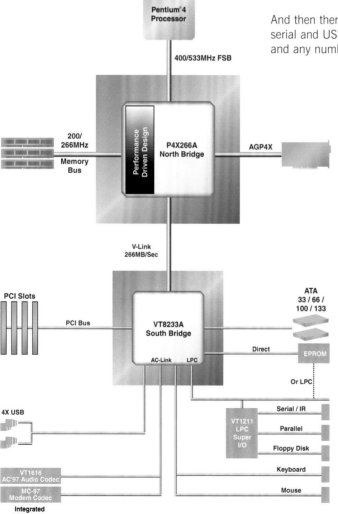

A chipset controls all the interfaces between components on a motherboard. Here we see a VIA chipset that illustrates the traditional North Bridge/South Bridge divide. Two chips split the main workload: North Bridge handles the fast processor, memory and AGP buses; and South Bridge – with the help of a supporting Super I/O chip – deals with everything else.

Bus bandwidths

Not all buses are equal. Far from it, in fact: they operate at different speeds and have different widths. For example, the basic single-speed (1x) AGP specification has a clock speed of 66MHz. This means that up to 66 million units of data can pass between the video card and the chipset in any single second. However, the AGP bus actually transfers 32 bits of data (32 individual 1s and 0s) with every clock cycle, so the true measure of the bus is not its speed alone but rather the overall rate at which data is transferred. This is known as the bandwidth of a bus. In this case, 32 bits pass through the bus 66 million times per second. This equates to a bandwidth of 266MB/sec.

Just to be clear here:

32 bits = 4 bytes, 66,000,000 x 4 = 264,000,000 bytes/sec.

There are 1,024 bytes in a kilobyte (KB), so this = 257,812KB/sec

There are 1,024 kilobytes in a megabyte (MB), so this = 252MB/sec

Which isn't the same as 266MB/sec at all! This is because a kilobyte is sometimes defined as 1,024 bytes and sometimes as 1,000 bytes. Uncertain convention dictates that the 1,000-byte approach is often used in the context of buses. Factor this into the equation above and the bandwidth becomes:

((66,000,000 x 4) / 1,000) / 1,000 = 264MB/sec

Closer. However, the true clock speed is actually 66.67MHz. Factor this in as well and we finally end up with a figure of (roughly) 266MB/sec.

The PCI bus is 133MB/sec and the old ISA bus maxed out at just over 8MB/sec. At the other extreme, the Front-Side Bus on a motherboard designed for a Pentium 4 processor is 64 bits wide and runs at either 400 or 533.33MHz. This equates to bandwidths, or data transfer rates, of 3,200MB/sec and 4,266MB/sec respectively. An Athlon XP FSB is also 64 bits wide but runs at 266.66MHz, making an overall bandwidth of 2,133MB/sec.

If all this makes your head spin, put away your calculator and consult the following table instead.

Some bus bandwidths

Bus	Bus speed (MHz)	Bus width (bits)	Data cycles*	Bandwidth (MB/sec)
PCI	33	32	1	133
AGP	66	32	1	266
AGP 2x	66	32	2	533
AGP 4x	66	32	4	1066
AGP 8x	66	32	8	2133
USB 1.1	12	1	1	1.5
USB 2.0	480	1	1	60
IEEE-1394	400	1	1	50
ATA-33	8.33	16	2	33
ATA-66	16.67	16	2	66
ATA-100	25	16	2	100
ATA-133	33	16	2	133
PC1600 DDR-RAM	100	64	2	1600
PC2100 DDR-RAM	133	64	2	2100
PC2700 DDR-RAM	166	64	2	2666
PC3200 DDR-RAM	200	64	2	3200
PC3700 DDR-RAM	233	64	2	3700
PC4000 DDR-RAM	250	64	2	4000
RIMM1600 RD-RAM (PC800)	400	16	2	1600**
RIMM 2100 RD-RAM (PC1066)	533	16	2	2132**
RIMM 3200 RD-RAM (PC800)	400	32	2	3200**
RIMM 4200 RD-RAM (PC1066)	533	32	2	4266**
RIMM 4800 RD-RAM (PC1200)	600	32	2	4800**
RIMM 6400 RD-RAM (PC800)	400	64	2	6400**
Pentium 4 FSB (400MHz)	100	64	4	3200
Pentium 4 FSB (533MHz)	133	64	4	4266
Pentium 4 FSB (800MHz)	200	64	4	6400
Athlon XP FSB (200MHz)	100	64	2	1600
Athlon XP FSB (266MHz)	133	64	2	2133
Athlon XP FSB (333MHz)	167	64	2	2666
Athlon XP FSB (400MHz)	200	64	2	3200

* Some buses transfer data two, four or more times on every clock cycle, which effectively doubles, quadruples etc. the overall bandwidth.

** RD-RAM modules can be used in a dual-channel configuration which effectively doubles the bandwidth once more.

Integrated video and audio, as featured in this ultra-mini motherboard, keeps the cost down. However, a motherboard that includes an AGP slot is a more flexible friend for the future than one without.

Integrated multimedia

Another important feature of motherboards that again depends upon the chipset is the presence or otherwise of 'onboard' or 'integrated' sound and/or video. An integrated sound chip means that the motherboard can handle audio playback and recording without the need for a separate sound card. That is, you simply connect speakers and a microphone to outputs and inputs provided by the motherboard. Similarly, integrated video means you don't need a separate video card.

The attraction of this approach is primarily one of reduced cost: a motherboard with integrated sound and/or video saves the system-builder having to shell out for one or two pricey expansion cards. A motherboard with integrated multimedia features is thus a smart buy, right?

Well, not necessarily. Remember, we're building the 'perfect PC' here, one requirement of which is that it must be able to adapt to your changing needs. The drawback with integrated multimedia is that it potentially limits your upgrade options. Audio is rather less of an issue than video. Sound cards are always designed for the PCI expansion slot so it's always possible to upgrade to a more powerful card later, assuming there is a free

slot on the motherboard. The slight complication is that you must disable the integrated sound chip before your sound card will work, as we'll see on p.113–114.

It is also possible to disable integrated video in favour of an expansion card – but where will you install it? Some motherboards with integrated video have a vacant AGP slot for just this purpose, in which case there's no problem: simply disable the chip and install your AGP expansion card. However, other motherboards, notably those based on Intel's 810 chipset, have no such slot, in which case you are, quite frankly, stuffed. Without a free AGP slot, your only real option would be to install a slower PCI video card, but this would almost certainly be a downgrade. Unless you are very, very confident that you will never wish to upgrade your PC's video capabilities – in particular, that you'll never play computer games or change from an analogue to a digital monitor or wish to run two monitors simultaneously – only consider a motherboard with integrated video if it also has a vacant AGP slot. A small saving now may have serious consequences later.

Intel now talks about hubs rather than bridges. But the MCH chip is basically a North Bridge and the ICH is a souped-up South Bridge that no longer requires a separate Super I/O chip.

Chipset architecture

We needn't linger on the physical design of chipsets except to comment briefly on the terminology you are likely to encounter:

North Bridge The primary chip in a chipset. It typically controls the processor, RAM, AGP and PCI buses.

South Bridge A second chip that typically incorporates the ISA, IDE and USB buses.

Super I/O A third, subsidiary chip that usually supports the floppy disk drive, serial ports and a parallel port, and sometimes also the mouse and keyboard ports.

However, these associations between bus and chip are far from immutable. Moreover, Intel recently switched to a 'hub architecture' where the North Bridge chip is called the Memory Controller Hub and the South Bridge is the I/O Controller Hub. AMD, that other processor-producing giant, refers to North Bridge and South Bridge chips as the System Controller and Peripheral Bus Controller respectively. From the buyer's perspective, it matters more what a chipset offers overall than how it does it.

QUICK Q&A

How do I identify a chipset? It isn't always that straightforward, particularly if you've picked up an old motherboard without documentation. The actual chips should carry their maker's mark, but the North Bridge chip will doubtless be concealed beneath a heatsink. If you know who made the motherboard and can locate the model number, a quick web search should reveal which chipset it uses. In fact, the motherboard manufacturer may itself maintain a support web page that hosts chipset drivers. Alternatively, Intel has a useful utility that can identify any Intel-made chipset, and the Sandra diagnostic tool from SiSoft can also reveal chipset information. See Appendix 3 for contact details.

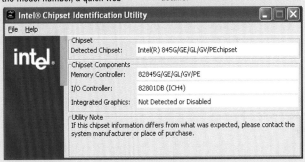

Intel's handy utility can pluck a chipset from the obscurity of a motherboard without lifting the covers.

Processor and memory support

The two most important questions with any chipset (and hence motherboard, and hence entire computer) are: which processor family does it work with and what kind of memory? For instance:

Chipset	Processor support	Memory support
VIA Apollo KT333	Athlon XP (Socket A)	DDR-RAM
Intel 845	Pentium 4 (Socket 478)	DDR-RAM
Intel 850	Pentium 4 (Socket 478)	RD-RAM

Now, the choice is somewhat simplified if you pick your processor first. For a Pentium 4 system, you need a motherboard with the Socket 478 design; if you want an Athlon XP-based system, you need a Socket A (also called Socket 462); and if you plump for an Athlon 64, look for Socket 754. Furthermore, if you opt for an Athlon XP, memory support is not an issue: all Socket A motherboards run DDR-RAM alone. But Pentium 4 motherboards can support either DDR-RAM or RD-RAM, so you need to settle upon your memory preference before shopping for the motherboard (yes, it is a little chicken-and-egg but these factors are all intricately intertwined). We'll consider processors and memory in detail shortly.

For now, here's a conundrum. Given two full-size ATX motherboards with the same chipset on sale at the same price, how do you choose between them? The devil, and the answer, is in the detail: not every manufacturer implements every aspect of a chipset's capabilities on every motherboard model. On seemingly identical motherboards, you may find that one has five PCI slots and one has six. How many USB ports do you get – two, four or six? Is there a digital output for relaying audio to an external recording device? Two, three or four memory slots? A spare fan connector in case you want to try your hand at over-clocking? A secondary BIOS for emergency use? A LAN port for easy networking? The list goes on …

See the summary pages on p.65–67 for a comprehensive checklist.

They don't look like very much, but between them these chips provide a motherboard with virtually all of its features.

TECHIE CORNER

Jumpers Many older motherboards use physical jumpers that control features like core voltage and the clock speed of the processor. These must be set correctly before you use the motherboard, which is not a problem if – and only if – you have the manual. Do be careful if you're intent on picking up a used model at a computer fair. Jumpers are a thing of the past on modern motherboards, thankfully, with such critical settings configured in and by BIOS.

Voltages and bus speeds can be controlled in BIOS or even with a software utility. However, this territory is usually reserved for over-clockers (i.e. geeks – sorry, but they are) desperate to squeeze a smidgen of extra performance from their processors.

PART 2 **Processor**

The processor, or CPU (Central Processing Unit), is of course your computer's 'brain'. It processes data at a phenomenal work rate and largely, but by no means solely, governs the overall performance of your PC. It is also the headline figure in most computer adverts, flagged up with a healthy dose of hyperbole:

'Blistering Speeds!'

'Unbelievable Performance!!'

'The Fastest Processor in the World … EVER!!!'.

You know the kind of thing. But the ads have a point, do they not? If you're building a new computer, surely you need the very fastest chip on the block?

You won't get far without a processor under the hood. Here we look at the options from Intel and AMD.

Speeds

In a word, no – or at least not unless you have very deep pockets indeed. Intel and AMD are the two main players in the processor market these days and both charge a remarkably hefty premium for the very latest models. The flipside of this equation is that earlier models attract a very healthy discount.

Here, for instance, are Intel's P4 prices on one completely random day. Note that these are trade prices based on boxes of 1,000 at a time, i.e. the price that an OEM would pay.

Pentium 4 model (GHz)	Price ($)
3.06	637
2.80	401
2.66	305
2.6	305
2.53	243
2.5	243
2.4	193
2.26	193
2.20	193

Here are AMD's OEM prices on the same day:

Athlon XP model	Price ($)
3000+	588
2800+	375
2700+	349
2600+	297
2400+	193
2200+	157

The actual prices are irrelevant – but just look at the differentials! A 2.66GHz P4 processor costs less than half that of a 3.06GHz model. A 2.4GHz costs $112 less again. What you have to ask yourself is whether you would actually notice the difference between, say, two billion clock cycles per second and three billion. In most cases – that is, short of running an incredibly processor-intensive application like real-time video-editing software – you simply wouldn't. Besides, is a 25% increase in performance really worth a 330% price premium? Remember, too, that you can always upgrade to a faster processor later when the price has fallen to a more realistic level. That 3.06GHz chip will cost under $200 some day soon.

Processor evolution

The history of CPUs is long, complicated and dull. Rather than discuss it at any great length, instead we present you with this table showing the current front-runners:

Pentium 4	Clock speed (GHz)[1]	L2 Cache (KB)[2]	FSB (MHz)	Socket
3.06	3.06	512	533	Socket 478
2.8	2.80	512	533	Socket 478
2.66	2.66	512	533	Socket 478
2.6	2.60	512	400	Socket 478
2.53	2.53	512	533	Socket 478
2.5	2.50	512	400	Socket 478
2.4/2.4B[3]	2.40	512	400/533	Socket 478
2.26	2.26	512	533	Socket 478
2.2	2.20	512	400	Socket 478
2.0 / 2.0A[4]	2.00	256/512	400	Socket 423/478
1.9	1.90	256	400	Socket 423/478
1.8 / 1.8A	1.80	256/512	400	Socket 423/478
1.7	1.70	256	400	Socket 423/478
1.6/1.6A	1.60	256	400	Socket 423/478
1.5	1.50	256	400	Socket 423/478
1.4	1.40	256	400	Socket 423/478

Athlon XP	Clock speed (GHz)	L2 Cache (KB)	FSB (MHz)	Socket
3000+ (Barton)[5]	2.17	512	333	Socket A
2800+ (Barton)	2.08	512	333	Socket A
2700+	2.17	256	333	Socket A
2600+	2.08	256	333	Socket A
2500+ (Barton)	1.83	512	333	Socket A
2400+	2.00	256	266	Socket A
2200+	1.80	256	266	Socket A
2100+	1.73	256	266	Socket A
2000+	1.67	256	266	Socket A
1900+	1.60	256	266	Socket A
1800+	1.53	256	266	Socket A
1700+	1.47	256	266	Socket A
1600+	1.40	256	266	Socket A
1500+	1.33	256	266	Socket A

Explanatory notes

1. Clock speed is a measure of a processor's work rate, expressed in millions (MHz) or billions (GHz) of cycles per second. Basically, the higher the clock speed, the more instructions a processor can carry out every second. However, the FSB and other key components in a computer system, notably memory, also affect how a processor performs in the real world. Clock speed is thus a guide to overall potential but by no means the end of the story.

2. Level 2 cache is a slither of extremely fast memory integrated within the processor. It acts as a buffer between the chipset and the processor and feeds the latter information at an extremely quick pace. More is merrier.

3. The 2.4GHz Pentium 4 is available with an optional 'B' suffix. This tells you that you're getting a processor with a fast 533MHz FSB rather than the same chip with a slower 400MHz bus.

4. Three P4 processors are available with an optional 'A' suffix, which tells you that they use Intel's smaller and more efficient 0.13-micron internal architecture (code-named Northwood) rather than the larger, less efficient 0.18-micron architecture (code-named Willamette). If opting for a 1.6, 1.8 or 2.0GHz processor, be sure to get an A model. All P4s from the 2.2GHz and beyond are all Northwoods, so the suffix has been dropped because there is no chance of confusion.

An AMD Athlon XP is slightly cheaper than a comparable Pentium 4, but it's certainly no slouch and certainly not a compromise. Rather, it's just a different building block.

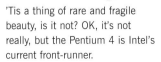

'Tis a thing of rare and fragile beauty, is it not? OK, it's not really, but the Pentium 4 is Intel's current front-runner.

5. AMD labelling is nothing if not contentious. Athlon XPs have a physically different structure from Pentium 4s, and AMD has long maintained that clock speed alone is not a true measure of a processor's potential. Thus it now brands each product with a '+' figure that relates to how it stacks up against a P4 with a similar clock speed. In other words, an Athlon XP 2400+ is reckoned to be broadly equivalent to a P4 2.4GHz despite having a clock speed of only 2GHz. Independent testing backs AMD's assertion, so we won't quibble.

Athlon XPs come with three different core architectures, known as Palomino, Thoroughbred and, most recently, Barton. What's 'interesting' is that the first crop of Barton chips – 2500+, 2800+ and 3000+ – are rated faster by AMD than Thoroughbred chips running at higher clock speeds. The Barton-built 2500+ Athlon XP, for instance, has a clock speed of only 1.83GHz compared with a Thoroughbred 2400+ running at 2GHz. The difference is in the cache: Barton processors have twice that of Thoroughbreds.

64-bit computing

Both Intel and AMD are now manufacturing 64-bit processors in the shape of the Itanium and Athlon 64 ranges respectively. But what does this mean for you?

Well, a 32-bit processor can process 232 individual blocks of information per clock cycle. Each block is in fact a byte, or a group of 8 bits, so this equates to 4.3 billion bytes, or 4GB. This in turn determines the maximum amount of RAM that the chip can 'address': any more RAM would simply be superfluous.

However, a 64-bit processor can process 264 bytes per clock cycle. In simplistic terms, this means it can handle many, many more instructions per second and work hand-in-hand with far greater quantities of RAM, thereby potentially improving system performance dramatically.

Which would be fine if your system performance needed dramatic improvement. The great limiting factor right now is the lack of operating system and application support for 64-bit processors. That is, unless and until Windows and your programs can actually take advantage of this new-found computational power, installing a 64-bit processor is like driving the archetypal Ferrari in a car park.

The short answer, then, is that 64-bit processors mean very little for you – for now. But watch this space, and expect to see software support develop rapidly.

TECHIE CORNER

Clock cycles The speed of everything on the motherboard is ultimately controlled by a tiny crystal that oscillates several million times every second when a current is applied. Bus speeds are either a multiple or sub-division of the crystal's frequency, or 'clock speed'.

CPU shopping with care

As we write, Pentium 4s are available with FSB speeds of 400MHz and 533MHz. You can still pick up Willamette models with the 0.18 micron internal architecture and, if you shop around, you might even find the odd Socket 423 model.

The important thing for the system-builder is to get a processor that is compatible with the latest motherboard architecture and chipset support. In the P4's case, this means a Socket 478 processor with a 533MHz FSB. The current top chip runs at 3,06GHz but costs a small fortune. For this project, we settled for a cheaper 2.4B Pentium 4 and a motherboard to match (see p.65-67). This processor will do all we ask of it today and could be easily swapped for a 3.06GHz or faster model tomorrow should we need a performance increase. It does not have Intel's much-vaunted HT Technology – see Techie Corner on p.33 – but the motherboard BIOS has built-in support for this so, again, our upgrade options are fully covered.

Potential purchasing mistakes would include:

- A motherboard that supports only the 400MHz FSB. All new P4 processors are now 533MHz and a further increase in bus speed is planned.

- A chipset that supports a 2.4GHz processor but nothing faster.

- A Socket 423 motherboard. This would limit your processor options to the sub-2.0GHz range with no possibility of an upgrade.

- A motherboard with a BIOS that is not HT Technology-ready. Although you might be able to slot in a 3.06GHz or faster P4, the computer would not be able to take advantage of its full potential without a corresponding BIOS update – a hassle that is easily and best avoided.

Budget buyers

You don't need to get a Pentium 4 or an Athlon XP, of course. For considerably less outlay, you could pick up an Intel Celeron or an AMD Duron processor. A Celeron is basically a low-cost, less-powerful P4 and a Duron is a budget Athlon. The main difference is that Celerons and Durons have less cache than their big brothers. Either will serve you very well indeed if your processing requirements are relatively limited.

Celerons in the 566MHz – 1.4GHz speed range use a Socket 370 design, but from 1.7GHz – 2.2GHz they use the same Socket 478 as all new P4s. Socket 370 motherboards are uncommon these days, and you could never replace a Socket 370 Celeron with a full-blown P4, so it makes more sense to choose a Socket 478-style Celeron.

Duron processors range from 1GHz to 1.3GHz and use the same Socket A design as the Athlon XP processor.

Here again are some OEM prices. Compare and contrast with the P4/Athlon XP pricing on p.29:

Celeron (GHz)	Price ($)
2.2	109
2.1	89
2	83
1.8	69
1.7	54

Duron (GHz)	Price ($)
1.3	47
1.2	42

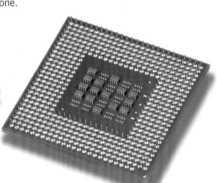

Spot the difference? A Celeron looks just like a P4 but carries a little less cache. This makes it a good option where price matters more than sheer performance alone.

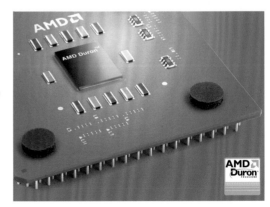

The Duron processor uses the same socket as the Athlon and, just like a Celeron, can save you big bucks, but is lacking in brawn.

They come in many shapes and sizes but, stylish or otherwise, a heatsink is an essential accoutrement for a hot CPU.

Cooling

Processors get very hot during use and need to be adequately cooled. This usually involves a heatsink unit with a built-in fan that attaches directly to the processor by means of clips. The heatsink has aluminium fins that dissipate heat generated by the hot core of the processor, and the fan cools it with a constant flow of air. Many motherboards also have a secondary heatsink to cool the North Bridge chip.

Without a heatsink, a processor would soon overheat and either shut itself down, if you are lucky, or burn out completely and probably take the motherboard with it.

All retail processors ship with suitable units in the box. Indeed, this is one very good reason to pay a little more for the retail packaging. If you source an OEM processor – i.e. one originally supplied to a computer manufacturer and later resold – you will also have to buy a compatible heatsink/fan. This is no great problem but do be sure to get one rated for the clock speed of your processor. It must also be designed for the appropriate socket, i.e. a Socket A heatsink won't fit in a Socket 478 motherboard.

We cover the installation of heatsinks in detail later. See also Appendix 1 on quiet PCs.

TECHIE CORNER

Hyper-Threading, or HT Technology, is a new feature of the very latest Pentium 4 processors. Essentially, it enables the chip to process multiple tasks simultaneously rather than sequentially. The result, Intel alleges, is a significant boost in performance during intensive multitasking, almost akin to having a second processor in your system. Indeed, HT specifically seeks to emulate the dual-processor environment that you might see in a top-end system designed to handle sustained number-crunching.

To see the benefits, you need both an HT-capable Pentium 4 processor and a chipset and BIOS that support the technology. However, the real-world benefits will vary according to what kind of software you use, and even which particular programs.

By the time you read this, HT Technology will probably be just another regular facet of the Pentium 4 generation. But right now the hype is high and the advantages remain largely unproven.

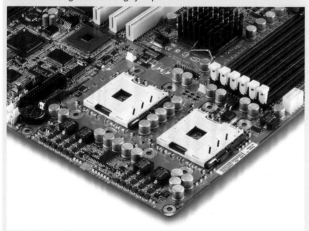

Hyper-Threading: the poor man's answer to a dual-processor motherboard.

QUICK Q&A

I thought some processors used slots on the motherboard instead of sockets?
They certainly used to, but no longer. Intel and AMD have both settled on a more efficient socket approach. Not that their processors use the same sockets as each other, of course; that would be just too easy.

You have to go back a bit to find slot-based processors but the second-hand buyer may fancy a high-end Pentium III or Athlon.

PART  **Memory**

System memory, or RAM, is just as critical a component in your new computer as the processor. More so, even. Too little memory and the fastest processor in the world will choke on its workload; stacks of memory and you can run several software applications at the same time without the system stuttering, hanging or crashing.

RAM comes in the form of chips soldered to long, thin modules that plug into slots on the motherboard. As mentioned above, any motherboard/chipset supports one type of RAM and one alone. This is not to say that you should buy your motherboard first and then look for compatible memory modules as an afterthought. Quite the reverse, in fact: as soon as you've decided between an Intel or an AMD processor, turn your thoughts to RAM and let this decision govern your choice of chipset (and hence motherboard).

Now, we could fill the rest of this manual with techie talk about memory evolution, error-checking, voltages, transistor counts and so forth, but it would (a) make your eyes glaze over and (b) get us almost nowhere. Let's focus instead on the absolute essentials.

Memory is running hotter and hotter these days, so much so that some of the latest DDR modules sport their very own heatsinks.

RD vs. DDR

When Pentium 4s first appeared, they were 'optimised' for a special kind of proprietary memory licensed (although not actually manufactured) by a company called Rambus. Called Rambus Dynamic RAM, or RD-RAM, the memory modules use a form factor known as RIMM and require corresponding RIMM slots on the motherboard. RIMMs come in 184-pin, 232-pin and 326-pin versions.

Athlon XP-based systems have always been built around an altogether different type of memory called Double Data Rate Synchronous Dynamic RAM, or DDR SD-RAM (we'll shorten this further to DDR-RAM). This comes in modules called DIMMs with 184 or 200 pins.

Speedwise, the bus between the memory slots and the chipset is extremely important as this dictates how quickly RAM modules can transfer data to and from the processor. In a perfect world, the memory bus and the processor bus (FSB) should be the same. Refer back to the bandwidth table on p.25 and note that RIMM 3200 RD-RAM memory has a bandwidth of 3,200MB/sec. So, too, does a P4 with a 400MHz FSB. The processor and memory modules are thus perfectly balanced to exchange data at the same high speed. Faster RIMM 4200 RD-RAM is equally matched to the faster 533MHz P4.

However, as non-proprietary DDR-RAM is generally cheaper than RD-RAM, and with Intel's initially strong support for RD-RAM appearing to be on the wane, we reckon that DDR-RAM has to be the better bet. Moreover, any difference in real-world performance between DDR-RAM and RD-RAM is, in our experience, so slight as to be virtually negligible.

QUICK Q&A

How much memory do I really need?
Well, Windows XP supports up to 4GB so that's the theoretical maximum. However, motherboards also have installation restrictions – for example, 2GB distributed through 3 DIMMs – so in practice you'll probably get nowhere near that. Generally, 512MB is about right for fairly demanding work, including audio and video processing. 256MB suffices for everyday office-style work, web browsing and so forth. Be guided by your software's minimum requirements, but be warned that these are often understated. If a program requires a nominal 64MB, you'll fare better with double that on-board. Much also depends upon how many tasks you run simultaneously on your PC, so close down unnecessary programs while using memory-hungry applications.

A 184-pin (count 'em) RIMM licensed by Rambus and made by Kingston. Rambus memory is hard to fault on raw performance terms but you do pay a hefty premium for the privilege.

Choosing your modules

Memory is manufactured in a truly mind-boggling array of specifications, making shopping for suitable modules a veritable nightmare. This is why we strongly recommend that you research and buy your motherboard first and check its memory support very carefully indeed. Then, to make life simpler, use one of the superb online memory configuration tools (see Appendix 3 for details). These will tell you exactly which modules are suitable.

There are 184 pins in this DIMM, just like the Rambus module earlier, but there similarities end. DDR memory is compatible with both Intel and AMD processors and poised to maintain its popularity with the introduction of Dual DDR modules.

Four simple rules

1) For a high-performance system, look for a chipset that supports the latest memory technology and bus speed. It may mean spending a little more but it guarantees an added measure of future-proofing. Older memory soon falls out of mass production.

2) Memory prices fluctuate wildly. If they are particularly high when you come to build your computer, consider settling for less than you'd really like at the outset and then upgrade as soon as prices plummet again (as they surely will).

3) Buy the fastest memory modules (i.e. highest bus speed) that your motherboard chipset supports. You might be able to use, say, 266MHz modules on a motherboard equipped with 333MHz DIMMs but it makes no sense to do so.

4) Don't skimp on RAM. Get enough. Get more than enough, in fact. You'll see far more benefits from an extra dollop of memory than from a faster processor or souped-up hard disk drive.

Sourcing memory modules

The motherboard that we eventually settled upon for this project (p.65) supports DDR-RAM running at either 266 or 333MHz. The manual makes clear that we need 184-pin 2.5V DIMMs. That's fine, but we wouldn't just wander into a superstore and expect to find something compatible leaping off the shelves. Rather, we looked it up.

TECHIE CORNER

SD-RAM Before DDR-RAM and RD-RAM, we had humble Synchronous Dynamic RAM. SD-RAM is dynamic because its contents are flushed continually and lost altogether when you turn off your computer; and it's synchronous because it is synchronised for performance with the motherboard's memory bus.

DDR-RAM is still synchronous and dynamic but it has double the bandwidth. Beyond that, Dual DDR (Dual Double Data Rate, believe it or not) memory is expected to arrive mid-2004. All of which shows, if it shows anything at all, that computer technology doesn't stand still for a moment. If you wait for the next development before making a purchase, you'll be hanging on till doomsday.

There are plenty of motherboards still around that support SD-RAM, but suitable memory modules are not quite so easy to obtain. Memory is a commodity market where demand drives supply and there's simply not much call for fresh SD-RAM these days. Still, the budget buyer prepared to shop around can do very nicely with a decent SD-RAM-compatible motherboard; after all, this type of memory served millions of PCs very nicely indeed between 1997 and 2001.

You can still get hold of SD-RAM for older motherboards but it's not exactly flying out of Taiwan's fabrication plants these days.

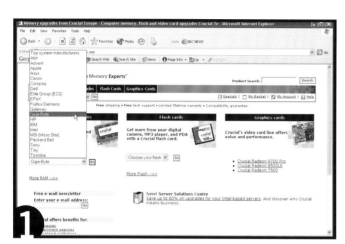

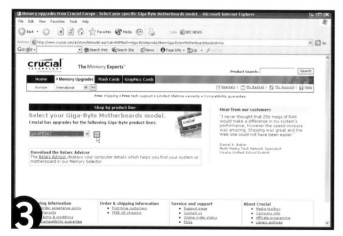

Crucial's online memory configuration utility prompts you first to select your motherboard manufacturer. In this case, it is Gigabyte. Select the relevant name from the popup list and click Go.

Now select the relevant product line and click Go again.

This generates an extremely long and gratifyingly comprehensive list of motherboards. Select yours with care.

Hey presto – a selection of compatible memory modules. We opted for a single 512MB module for this project.

PART  **Case**

Just as all motherboards adhere to certain industry-standard dimensions, so do computer cases. Far and away the most common form factor is, again, ATX. You can be sure that any ATX-style motherboard will fit in any ATX-style case.

A full-sized tower case offers
space, flexibility and almost
unlimited expansion possibilities.
Then again, it's absolutely huge. A
mid-tower is often a fair
compromise.

Towers vs. desktops

Which is not to say that all cases are the same. Far from it, in fact. For starters, you can choose between a tower case or a desktop case. One is tall and narrow, the other squat and wide. We heartily recommend going for a tower case. They are overwhelmingly more prevalent than desktop cases and, in our experience, considerably easier to work with.

You can also get mid- and mini-tower cases which are progressively shorter versions of a full-tower case. The sole advantage of a low-rise tower is neatness; the considerable disadvantage is a corresponding lack of expansion possibilities. A mini-tower will typically have two or three 5.25-inch drive bays, a mid-tower between three and five, and a full-tower anywhere up to seven. Given that you will probably install a CD-RW drive and a DVD-ROM drive, a three-bay case still has room for one additional device (a tape drive, perhaps, or a sound card's breakout box, or a drive-mounted USB hub). You should aim to have at least one spare drive bay.

Pay attention to 3.5-inch drive bays, too. You'll need one for the hard disk drive and another for the floppy drive. Again, a spare bay is valuable. A tall tower case is also essential if you want to install a silent heatsink (see p.130).

Case features

Drive bays are protected by drive bay covers on the front of the case. These snap-out or unscrew to afford full access to the bay, whereupon you can install an internally-mounted drive.

A case also has a series of blanking plates to the rear that correspond to the motherboard's PCI and AGP slots. You'll remove one every time you install an expansion card.

Towards the top of the tower is a rectangular input–output (I/O) panel. This is where the mouse, keyboard, parallel, serial and other ports will poke through when the motherboard is installed. You'll get an I/O shield supplied with the case but the chances are that it won't correspond to your motherboard's connectors. No matter – motherboards always ship with a compatible I/O shield in the box.

On the front of the case, you will find two buttons: the main power on/off switch and a smaller, usually recessed reset button that restarts your computer if Windows hangs. There will be a couple of lights, too: one to show when the power is on, and one that flickers whenever the hard disk drive is particularly active.

The case may also have an extra opening that can accommodate an expansion bracket loaded with audio or USB ports. Such a bracket would be supplied with the motherboard so, again, it pays to get the motherboard first and use it as the basis for all other purchases.

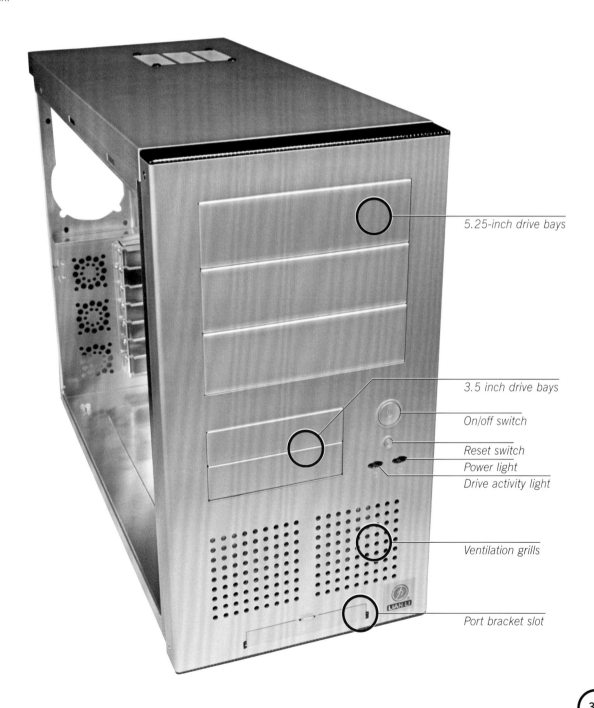

5.25-inch drive bays

3.5 inch drive bays

On/off switch

Reset switch

Power light

Drive activity light

Ventilation grills

Port bracket slot

Your case may have a handy removable tray to which you can attach the motherboard, or it may require you to screw the motherboard directly to the chassis. We highly recommend the tray approach for ease of use – not that we got one for this project, mind – but it does tend to bump up the price.

Inside the case, there may be mounting for an extra air-intake fan or two, and there should certainly be at least one pre-installed fan. The case will also have a speaker which the BIOS will use to generate beeps (see p.132). Finally, you may find a separate internal cage that could hold a further two or more 3.5-inch drives – essential for a RAID system (see p47).

Beyond all of this, designs vary from the standard, boring 'big beige box' look to undeniably funky. Pressed-steel cases are generally cheaper but brushed-aluminium looks (and stays) cooler. Some cases are heavy, reinforced and thoroughly sturdy; others are lightweight, flimsy and easily dented. Some cases have side panels secured with thumbscrews for easy access, others would try the patience of a contortionist.

We would simply advise you to focus on functionality before frills. A full-sized tower case is generally easier to work with, easier to keep tidy internally, more adaptable to customisation and provides better airflow to the motherboard's components.

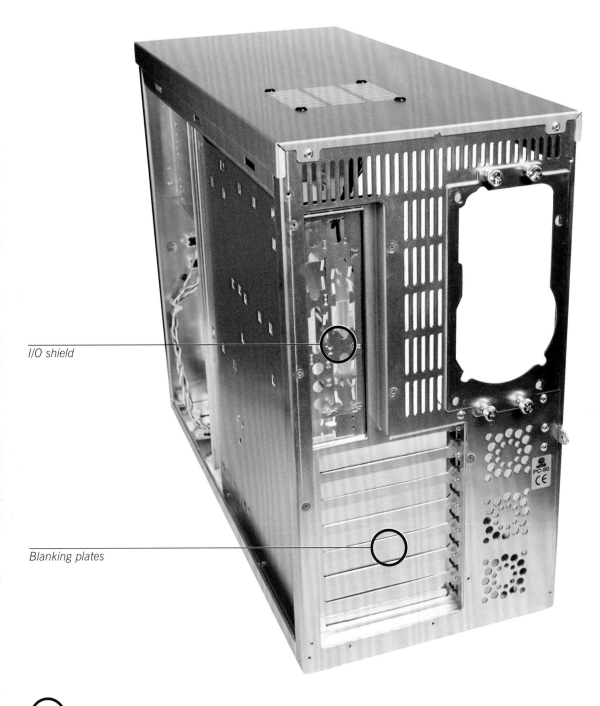

I/O shield

Blanking plates

With the side panels removed, here we see the 5.25-inch and 3.5-inch drive bays from within. Attached to the floor of the case is an additional cage that could accommodate two more hard disk drives. Note, too, the air intake fan sited behind the ventilation grills.

Looking towards the rear of the case, we see the removable blanking covers that allow expansion cards to reach the outside world. The big hole is for the power supply unit and, above that, on the roof, is a second internal fan.

PART  Power supply

The power supply unit (PSU) supplies power to the computer's motherboard and drives. That much is obvious. Less so is the importance of getting the right PSU, particularly when many cases come with an anonymous unit pre-installed. Ignore the specs here and you risk all sorts of problems.

A reliable power supply is a must. This ATX model has adjustable fan speed – strictly non-essential but helps to keep the noise down – and pumps out up to 350W. It also complies with AMD's stringent design requirements (see Techie corner box opposite).

Form factor

To go with your ATX case and ATX motherboard, you need an ATX PSU. Virtually all new PSUs comply with the ATX standard, but do be careful when buying second-hand. If the labelling is unclear, check the main motherboard connector. Old AT-style PSUs connect to the motherboard with a pair of plugs that have six wires apiece (see p.92); ATX PSUs use a single 20-pin plug.

It is possible to get an adapter that enables an AT-style PSU to power an ATX motherboard but we don't recommend it. In fact, we don't really recommend buying a second-hand PSU at all. An under-powered PSU might not supply power-hungry components with the juice they need, particularly if you cram your case full of drives and accessories, and an older unit with a history of hard work behind it is obviously more liable to burn out and die.

Power rating

A 250W PSU is inadequate; 300W is fine; 350W is better still. Simple as that.

ATX Auxiliary

A 6-pin power connection required by some motherboards. If your motherboard has an ATX Auxiliary socket, you must use it, which means you must get an ATA Auxiliary-equipped PSU.

ATX 12V

Pentium 4 motherboards require yet another cable connection from the PSU. An ATX 12V plug has four wires and usually connects to a socket near the processor. Again, any motherboard that has an ATX 12V socket must be powered by an ATX 12V PSU.

Drive connectors

The PSU connects directly to every internal drive in your PC. There are two types of cable and plug, each with four wires/pins. The larger 'Molex' style is used to power optical and hard disk drives, and the smaller 'Berg' plug powers the floppy drive. You might just get away with three large plugs and one small, as this would let you run one hard disk drive, one CD drive, one DVD drive and a floppy drive. However, most PSUs have several spare cables.

ATX power connector

ATX auxiliary

ATX 12V

Molex

Berg

TECHIE CORNER

Cooling AMD is very particular about cooling and airflow requirements. In particular, it recommends the use of a PSU with an air intake on the bottom of the unit, i.e. in the vicinity of the processor. You can find a list of accredited PSUs on AMD's website (www.amd.com).

	Desirable Version	Undesirable Version	
Rear:			They look about the same! (Differences are brand specific)
Front			Intake only in front is not optimal
Bottom			Bottom intake cools the CPU best

If you're using an Athlon XP processor, don't assume that just any old PSU will do; AMD lays down specific requirements and you'd best buy a unit that abides by them.

Cooling

A PSU has an integrated fan that controls air-flow through the computer case. Some also have a second fan that blows cool air at the motherboard. We strongly recommend that you buy a PSU specifically rated for a P4 or Athlon XP system (whichever applies to you).

Noise

A secondary consideration, certainly, but important nonetheless. Some PSUs make a terrible racket while others operate with barely a whisper. If a peaceful PC is important to you, shop around for a quiet device with adjustable-speed fans. See also Appendix 1.

And so ...

To sum up, your ATX PSU should have:

- 300–350W output.
- A single 20-pin motherboard connector.
- An ATX Auxiliary connector (possibly not required by your motherboard but good to have anyway).
- An ATX 12V connector (required for Pentium 4 motherboards).
- An absolute minimum of five drive connectors (three large and two small).

Hard disk drive

You'll want to install a decent-sized hard disk drive (HDD) in your computer but that could mean anything from 40GB to 120GB or more. Digital video, image and sound files certainly eat heavily into disk space, but the truth is that few people ever come close to filling today's monster drives. Besides, you can always add a second internal or external HDD later if you run out of room. Non-essential material can also be easily archived on CD-R media to free up disk space as and when required. We'll focus here on other concerns beyond mere storage.

Interface

The two abbreviations you'll come across most frequently are IDE (Integrated Drive Electronics, sometimes prefixed with an extra E for Enhanced) and ATA (Advanced Technology Attachment). Although technically distinct, these terms are used interchangeably to describe the connection between the HDD and the motherboard.

Another common abbreviation is DMA (Direct Memory Access, sometimes prefixed with an extra U for Ultra). This tells you that the device can 'talk' to RAM directly without sending data through the processor first – a good thing.

And then there's ATAPI, which is ATA with a Packet Interface bolted on. This means that optical CD and DVD drives can use the same interface as the HDD.

In most cases, the motherboard comes with a pair of IDE/ATA connectors labelled IDE1 and IDE2, each of which can support one or two devices. IDE1 provides the Primary channel, to which you would typically connect the hard disk drive; and IDE2 provides the Secondary channel, to which you would typically connect the CD and DVD drives.

The IDE-ATA interface has evolved over time but, as so often, the names applied to the various standards are neither transparent nor particularly helpful. Use this table for reference:

Interface	Also know as	Maximum bandwidth (MB/sec)
ATA-66	ATA-5, IDE-66 or UDMA-66	66MB/sec
ATA-100	ATA-6, IDE-100 or UDMA-100	100MB/sec
ATA-133	ATA-7, IDE-133 or UDMA-133	133MB/sec

Our project motherboard supports the ATA-100 interface so we would be unwise to use a slower ATA-66 drive. However, there would be no point installing an ATA-133 drive either, as it would (in theory anyway – see below) be restricted by the motherboard interface.

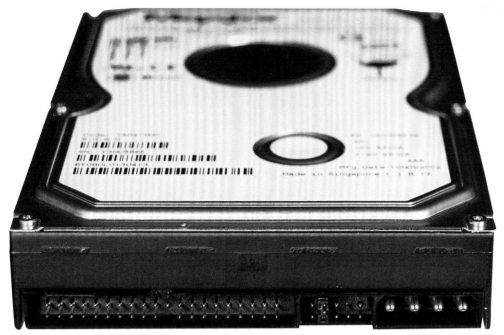

Hard disk drives now routinely top 80GB. That's a phenomenal amount of storage space when you think about it, particularly when you can archive up to 700MB of files at a time on a single recordable CD. Don't feel obliged to go overboard. Here, from left to right, we can see the IDE/ATA ribbon cable socket, the jumper pins and the 4-pin power cable socket.

Data transfer rates

The real-world performance of a drive doesn't just depend on the bandwidth. In fact, many an ATA-100 drive can outpace an ATA-133 device at reading or saving large files. It comes down to a specification called the internal, or sustained, transfer rate. This is a measure of how quickly a drive can read data from its own disks. The bandwidth figures quoted above relate to the external transfer rate but this merely tells you how quickly the drive can shift data out to the main system. Manufacturers are notoriously reticent about sustained transfer rates, one reason being that the figure is significantly lower than the headline-grabbing external interface.

Sustained transfer rates peak between around 40–70MB/sec, which is some way short of even the ATA-100 standard's external transfer rate. The drive may be perfectly capable of pumping out huge volumes of data but this is of questionable value if it can't gather this data at anything like the same rate. The bottleneck is the drive itself, not the interface.

Serial ATA

One important recent development is the emergence of Serial ATA, or SATA. This promises to increase the bandwidth of the HDD bus to 150MB/sec initially and then well beyond into the realms of 300 and 600MB/sec. One welcome change for system-builders is a new cable design: SATA uses a thin, flexible cable instead of the current flat ribbon-style cable. This is neater and better for airflow around the case. However, while sustained transfer rates within drives remain significantly lower than the external interface, the impact of SATA in terms of raw performance is likely to be marginal.

Serial ATA is coming to a computer near you soon: skinny cables, greater bandwidth and no more of this Master/Slave nonsense either.

Cables

For an ATA-66 or faster HDD, use only an 80-conductor IDE/ATA cable. This has the same plugs as the older 40-conductor style and looks very similar, but it incorporates twice as many wires within the ribbon. The extra wires are essentially non-functional, but they reduce interference and help preserve a true signal.

Two drives sharing an IDE/ATA channel on the motherboard must be allocated Master and Slave status in order that the motherboard can tell them apart. This is achieved with little plastic jumpers. If you mistakenly set both drives to either Master or Slave, neither will work. However, with an 80-conductor cable you can set all drives to the Cable Select position and forget about them: the cable sorts out Master/Slave status automatically (see also p.100).

Other specs

Some other HDD specs to be aware of include:

Cache A slice of memory built into the drive that holds frequently accessed data in a buffer state. This saves the drive having to continually re-read from its disks. A 2MB cache is a good minimum.

Spindle speed The rate at which the drive's disks spin. This has a bearing on how quickly the device can read and write data. 5,400rpm is adequate for a low-spec system but we'd recommend a 7,200rpm drive. As a not-entirely-consistent rule, a 7,200rpm drive will have a faster sustained transfer rate than a 5,400rpm drive.

S.M.A.R.T. An error-checking procedure that tries to predict when a hard disk drive has an increased risk of failing in the near future. This gives you time to make a critical data backup. You need two things: a S.M.A.R.T.-enabled drive and either a motherboard BIOS with native support for S.M.A.R.T. or a standalone software program that works in tandem with the drive.

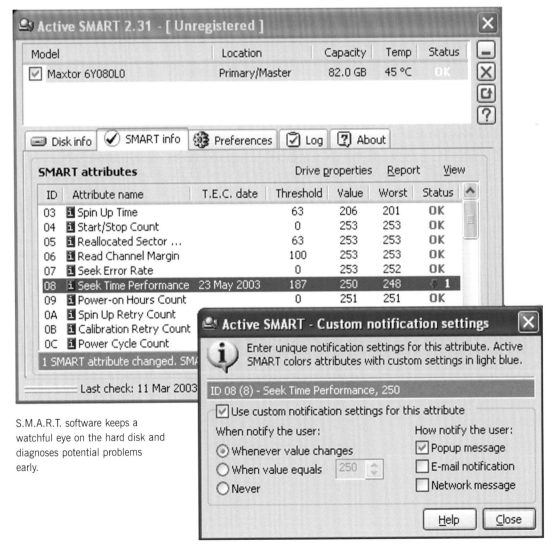

S.M.A.R.T. software keeps a watchful eye on the hard disk and diagnoses potential problems early.

Hard disk drive limitations The history of hard disk drive evolution is marked, even marred, by a sequence of limitations that made it difficult or even impossible to use high-capacity drives. The three most important limitations are:

8.4GB A BIOS limitation that affects most motherboards manufactured before 1998. Simply put, an old BIOS won't recognise any drive that's bigger than 8.4GB. A BIOS update, if available, can sometimes put matters right.

32GB Windows 95 recognises drives up to but not beyond 32GB. This is quite easily overcome by installing Windows 98 or beyond.

137.4GB It sounds a lot but it's not beyond the realms of possibility that you would want to install, say, a 160GB drive in your new computer. However, the IDE/ATA specification itself supports disks of only up to 137.4GB and most BIOS programs made pre-2002 baulk at anything bigger. Again, a BIOS update and/or a recent motherboard are your best bet.

RAID

Once the preserve of network servers, a RAID (Redundant Array of Independent Disks) setup is now a possibility for many home/office computers. Essentially, a RAID-supporting motherboard lets you use two or more hard disk drives simultaneously to 'stripe' or 'mirror' data.

With striping, also called RAID Level 0, the computer treats each hard disk as part of a whole. Two 60GB drives, for example, effectively become a single 120GB drive. Data is then distributed evenly between (or among) the drives, resulting in faster read/write performance. The risk is that a single drive failure means all data is lost.

With mirroring, or RAID Level 1, every file you save to the primary hard disk is simultaneously copied to every other drive in the system. Such duplication offers a high level of data security and reliability but, because the additional drives simply mirror the contents of the primary drive, you don't get the benefits of additional storage capacity. It's an expensive way to safeguard your files.

If you reckon RAID is for you, look for a chipset/motherboard with RAID drive controllers and RAID-compatible BIOS. Some motherboards support striping and mirroring simultaneously (Level 0+1), although for this you would need a grand total of four drives..

RAID offers additional storage space or security or, if you install four hard drives, both. Kits like this let you use external hard drives connected through a SCSI interface – ideal if your motherboard has only two IDE controllers, but hardly a cheap option.

PART 2

Sound card

Before buying a sound card, ask yourself four questions:

- Do you want to play music on your computer?
- Do you want to play games on your computer?
- Do you want to watch movies on your computer?
- Do you want to record music on your computer?

The answers determine what kind of sound card you need.

A sound card like Creative Labs Audigy 2 has more bells and whistles built in to it than many an entire computer of yesteryear. Essential equipment for the musician or gamer but only true audiophiles get really worked up about the nuances of one sound technology over another.

Music

For music playback, be it audio CD tracks, MP3 files or any other format, stereo is usually sufficient. Most music even today is still recorded in stereo so adding a few extra speakers here and there doesn't actually enhance the sound.

Games

Here you'll benefit from a surround sound system. This is where the audio signal is composed of several discrete channels relayed to satellite speakers strategically positioned around the listener. Most games have four-channel soundtracks, so you need a 4.1 speaker set-up for best effect (front left, front right, rear left, rear right, plus a separate subwoofer for bass frequencies) and a sound card that can decode the signal.

The sound card should also support one or more of the popular sound technologies, including DirectSound3D, THX, A3D and particularly EAX. The trouble is – as you will know if you've ever given this field more than a cursory glance – that there are so many competing, evolving and incompatible standards out there that it's simply impossible to (a) get a sound card that supports everything, and (b) keep up! Still, just about every game will play in a fallback DirectX mode, and should even install the requisite software for you.

Movies

DVD movie soundtracks are almost always encoded in 5.1 surround sound with either Dolby Digital or DTS technology. To hear this to full advantage, you need an additional speaker positioned directly in front of you. You also need a sound card that can either decode the signal itself or pass it through to a separate decoder unit that sits between the card and the speakers.

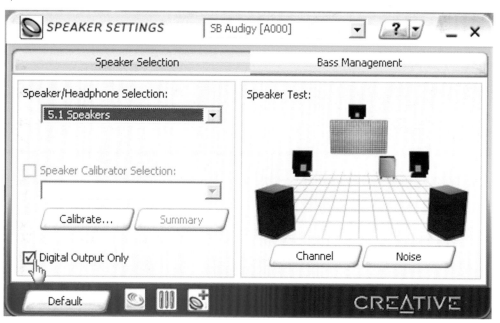

Fancy a cinema in your sitting room? Then you'll need a 5.1 surround sound-capable card with a speaker system to match.

Recording

Should you wish to connect a MIDI keyboard or other controller
to your computer, you'll need a MIDI input. This is pretty much
standard; most sound cards provide a combined MIDI/games
controller port. Look for ASIO support, too. This is a driver
standard that reduces the delay, or latency, between, for example,
pressing a key on a MIDI keyboard and the sound registering
with the recording software. Latency used to make multi-track
recording a real pain, but ASIO drivers help enormously.

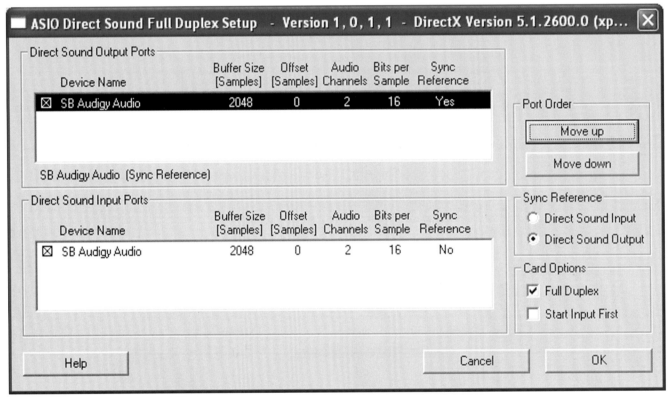

ASIO drivers were developed by
sound specialist Steinberg to
reduce latency and improve MIDI
recording.

Integrated vs. expansion card

Our motherboard came with 5.1 audio provided by an integrated AC '97-compliant chip. AC '97 is an Intel-specified industry-wide standard that guarantees high-quality multi-channel audio output; perfect for games, movies, music and, of course, the everyday bells and whistles generated by web pages and Windows.

The main disadvantage with integrated audio is that you only get a limited number of inputs and outputs – typically a few on the I/O panel and perhaps an optional port bracket – and you may have to fiddle with software settings in order to connect the full array of speakers.

Integrated multi-channel audio has advanced to the point where it rivals expansion cards in almost every area. Only the musician or someone with very particular connectivity requirements really need look further. However, in this project we will install a separate sound card to illustrate how to disable the integrated audio chip.

When you don't have enough ports to connect lots of satellite speakers, something has to give. Here, with an integrated sound chip on the motherboard and only three audio ports provided on the I/O panel (p.22), a software driver rings the changes in order to enable 5.1 output. The blue line-in port changes function to rear speakers out, and the red microphone-in port now handles the centre and subwoofer channels.

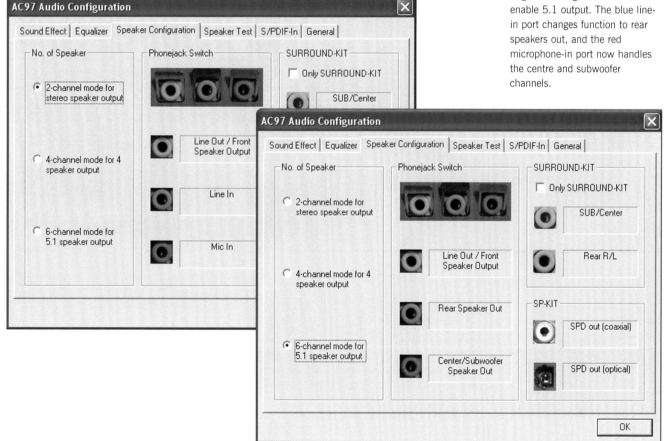

PART  Video card

Like sound technology, the computer graphics arena is a fast-moving, ever-shifting, highly-competitive minefield of acronyms, abbreviations and indecipherable, incompatible 'standards'. Anything we say now will be out of date by the end of the day, if not the paragraph.

It's 'only' a video card, but a powerful beast like this Nvidia Ti model needs its own on-board cooling system and a fast AGP slot to do it justice. Note that hook on the bottom edge. This is essential to secure the heavy card to the motherboard, as we shall see later (p.105).

Chipsets

Just as a motherboard is built around a chipset, so a video card (or graphics card, as they are also called) has at its heart a Graphics Processing Unit (GPU). This is supported by a hefty slice of dedicated RAM located on the card itself. In effect, the video card is like a mini-computer in its own right, albeit with the very specific task of generating images on a monitor screen.

The two main GPU players right now are Nvidia and ATI. Neither company actually makes its own video cards but they have the OEM business pretty well stitched up, so any card you buy is likely to feature an Nvidia or an ATI chip regardless of its brand. Keep an eye on the latest Matrox cards, too, especially if you need multiple monitor support (see Quick Q&A on p.54).

2D/3D

All you need for a two-dimensional display at a comfortable resolution of 1,024 x 768 pixels is a mere 4MB of on-card memory. That's fine for office applications, image editing, web browsing and pretty much everything else. However, computer games demand a lot of additional oomph. 32MB is about the minimum, but you'll find most cards now have 64 or 128MB of RAM.

3D isn't really three-dimensional, of course, but the card uses complex lighting and texture techniques to create a realistic illusion of depth.

Interface

AGP (Accelerated Graphics Port) is a special slot on the motherboard with double the bandwidth of PCI. It is specifically reserved for video cards. You can still get PCI video cards, of course, which are just fine for 2D work. But AGP is preferable, and often essential, if you want to play the latest games.

Beyond single-speed AGP, we find 2x, 4x and even 8x enhancements with correspondingly greater bus bandwidths. The serious gamer should go for both the fastest bus and the most memory available.

We said earlier that we are reluctant to recommend integrated video unless the motherboard also has a free AGP slot, and we reiterate that now. It simply doesn't make sense to rule out future upgrades from the outset. The one possible exception is the emerging nForce 2 chipset from Nvidia, where superb integrated video is at the heart of the chipset rather than a mere afterthought. Currently it's available only on Athlon XP motherboards.

QUICK Q&A

I've just been reading up on computer game standards and now my head hurts. What should I do?
Buy a PlayStation2? Sorry to sound flippant but computer gaming gives us a headache too. With a games console, you know that any game designed for that particular platform – PlayStation, Xbox, GameCube or whatever – will work straight out of the box with no configuration. Which is not to say that we are anti-computer gaming; it's just that we prefer the simplicity of a dedicated gaming platform, just as we'd rather watch a DVD movie on a television screen than a monitor.

A PCI video card is not necessarily to be sneezed at if all you want to do is hook up a monitor and run 2D applications.

DVI

A video card is a natively digital device that has to perform a digital-to-analogue conversion in order that an analogue monitor can make sense of its output signal. This conversion degrades the integrity of the signal to a degree (a small degree, admittedly). Worse, modern flat-panel TFT monitors are actually digital devices at heart, so the analogue signal has to be re-converted back to digital upon receipt. This is patently crazy, hence the evolution of a purely digital connection between video card and monitor: DVI (Digital Visual Interface).

When you connect a DVI monitor to a DVI video card, the digital signal is transferred from one to the other more or less wholesale. The result is a truer image with more faithful colour representations. Better still, there's no need to mess around with fiddly monitor controls in pursuit of a perfect picture: the card and monitor work in harmony to display the best possible image automatically.

The traditional 15-pin VGA plug and socket will eventually disappear in favour of DVI so a DVI-capable video card is a sensible purchase. Digital monitors still carry a premium price, however, so you may wish to use a cheaper analogue monitor in the meantime. A simple DVI-to-VGA adapter is all you need to connect it to the card.

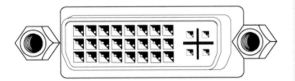

If your video card has only one port, make sure that it's DVI-I rather than DVD-D. A DVI-I port has five additional pins over and above DVD-D's 24 pins, which means it can be used (with an adapter) to run an analogue monitor. Alternatively, some cards have both DVD-D and VGA ports, which keeps your options similarly open.

QUICK Q&A

My video card has both VGA and DVI ports. Can I connect two monitors?
Probably not. Many video cards provide two outputs, but these are mere alternatives, i.e. you can use one port or the other but not both simultaneously. If you want to run two monitors, the usual approach is to install a PCI video card alongside the AGP card and connect one monitor to each. Windows recognises this arrangement automatically so configuration is straightforward.

However, you can also get 'dual-head' and 'triple-head' video cards that incorporate all the circuitry required to run two or three monitors through the same bus. This is actually preferable because (a) you get an AGP-generated display on each monitor and (b) it doesn't eat into your allocation of PCI slots.

For the best results with multiple-monitor displays, invest in a specialist card like the Matrox Parhelia. One DVI channel can be split to run two monitors, meaning that up to three can be powered simultaneously from a single AGP interface.

One thing to watch: Pre-1998 motherboards equipped with 1x or 2x speed AGP ports can only use video cards that operate at 3.3V. Newer slots and cards are designed to run at 1.5V, so don't assume that you can install any old AGP video card in a new motherboard – or indeed that you can install a new card in an old motherboard.

And another: it looks like the AGP bus is poised to be superseded altogether in 2004/5 (for which read 2006/7) by a new interface imaginatively entitled PCI Express. This will boost the bandwidth to 4GB/sec and beyond (equivalent to 16x AGP).

DVD decoding

To watch DVD movies on your computer, you will need both a DVD-ROM drive to play the disc and a video card that can decode the encoded movie file. Look for MPEG-2 decoding; almost a given these days, but not quite. If you get sold short, your options are to use a separate MPEG-2 decoder expansion card (extra expense and requires a PCI slot) or to rely upon software decoding (i.e. a movie player program that decodes the movie on the fly). Software decoding is fine with a fast processor but Celerons and Durons may not keep pace, resulting in jerky playback.

Optional extras

These include:

TV-out This lets you hook up your computer to a TV set instead of a monitor.

Dual-monitor support Connect two monitors simultaneously for a widescreen effect.

TV tuner Plug in an aerial to bring the small screen to you monitor.

Buy a video card with a built in TV tuner to watch and even record television programmes on your computer.

Optical drives

The 'average' shop-bought PC these days has two optical drives: a CD-RW drive and a DVD-ROM drive. Some come with single 'combo' drives instead that combine CD-RW and DVD-ROM functionality within a single device. You, of course, can have whatever you like.

Interface

If your motherboard has two ATA/IDE controllers, as is the norm, you can connect two devices to each. Typically you would install the HDD on the motherboard's primary channel (IDE1) and have your CD and DVD drives share the secondary channel (IDE2).

You don't need to use 80-conductor cables with optical drives (see p.46) but it does no harm and gives you the useful option of being able to set the jumpers on both devices to Cable Select.

To install more than four drives, perhaps for a RAID setup or to use multiple optical drives, you would first have to equip the motherboard with an additional IDE interface. This is easily achieved with a PCI expansion card. Or, of course, you can use external drives that connect through USB or FireWire ports.

Looking at a typical drive from a less flattering angle, from left to right we see the digital (small) and analogue (larger) audio cable sockets, the jumper pins, the IDE/ATA ribbon cable socket and finally the 4-pin Molex power socket.

TECHIE CORNER

CD and DVD capacity The technical differences between CD and DVD technology are many and microscopic, although you wouldn't think so from appearance alone. But the practical difference is really just one of storage space. A CD can hold between 650 and 700MB of data but DVDs start at 4.37/4.7GB and, in the double-sided, dual-layer format, reach all the way up to 15.9/17.1GB.

The either/or figures are because of an eternal confusion over what a Gigabyte actually is in the context of DVDs: either 1,073,741,824 bytes or 1,000,000,000 bytes, depending who you ask. The higher capacity figures (4.7 and 17.1GB) are based on the straight 'billion bytes' definition. On a computer, however, one Gigabyte of data is always defined as 1,024 x 1,024 x 1,024 bytes (= 1,073,741,824 bytes). The net result is that a data Gigabyte is bigger than a DVD Gigabyte. The consequence? – you can only fit 4.37GB of computer files on a 4.7GB DVD.

If you settle for a CD-RW and DVD-ROM drive at the outset, you can always add an external DVD writer later.

CD & DVD

A plain CD-ROM drive can read and play CDs but a CD-RW drive lets you make your own. There are two types of media: CD-R discs that, once full, cannot be erased or re-recorded; and CD-RW discs that can be reused time and time again.

To read DVD discs, be they data, audio or movie, you need a DVD-ROM drive. But if you want to make your own DVDs, you need a DVD writer – and that's where the fun begins …

Recording/writing/burning (one and the same) your own audio, data, video or whatever CDs is a breeze. Windows XP supports basic CD recording without the need for any third-party software, and all told it's the cheapest, most efficient way to back up important files.

Recordable DVD

The current state of play is a commercial shambles and looks like continuing in the same vein for some time to come. Essentially, there are three competing, incompatible recording technologies: DVD-R/-RW, DVD+R/+RW and DVD-RAM. Each has its pros, its cons, its proponents and its detractors. Three points:

- To backup and safeguard your own files, any format will do just fine. You needn't worry about compatibility issues if sharing your discs is not an issue.

- To turn a video file into a DVD movie that you can watch on the DVD player in your living room, check which recordable DVD technology the player can read (if any) and buy a drive to match. DVD-R/-RW has the widest drive/player compatibility, DVD+R/+RW appears to be growing in popularity and DVD-RAM is compatible with very few DVD players.

- Better still, buy a recordable drive that supports all recording formats. These are now widely available and can help you work around any compatibility problems.

A recordable DVD drive looks just like a CD drive but there's a power of technology packed into that case. Unfortunately, one technology resolutely does not suit all.

Speed

CD-RW drives carry speed ratings which refer, rather imprecisely, to their read and write speeds. The very first generation of CD-ROM drives read data at a top rate of 150KB/sec. Faster speeds are expressed as a multiple of this speed: 2x, 4x and so on. For instance, a 40x-speed drive can read data at 6,000KB/sec.

Drives are at their slowest when writing (or recording – it means the same thing) data to CD-RW media, but the newer models can record to CD-R media almost as, or just as, quickly as they can read data. Thus a drive billed as 48/40/12x reads at 48x-speed, writes to CD-R media at 40x-speed and writes to CD-RW media at 12x.

DVD-ROM drives are also speed-rated. However, the base speed here is 1,385KB/sec, which is about nine times faster than an original CD drive. A 16x-speed DVD drive thus reads data at a rate of over 21MB/sec. Not that you really need this kind of speed in everyday use; a 1x DVD drive is adequate for movie playback.

Internal optical drives, be they CD or DVD, ROM or RW, use the 5.25-inch drive bay and are all fully compatible with the IDE/ATA channels on the motherboard.

MultiRead

One specification well worth looking at is a drive's MultiRead capability. This pertains to a couple of standards intended to ensure compatibility between drives and different types of media.

A CD drive that carries the MultiRead logo must be able to read all of the following formats:
- CD-DA (audio CD)
- CD-ROM
- CD-R
- CD-RW

A DVD drive carrying the MultiRead2 logo must be able to read all of the above but also read these formats:
- DVD-ROM
- DVD-Video
- DVD-Audio
- DVD-RAM

So, for instance, you can make your own CD-R or CD-RW discs and be certain that they will play in any MultiRead or MultiRead2 drive.

QUICK Q&A

Should I consider a 'combo' drive?

By all means. A combo drive is effectively a CD-RW and DVD-ROM drive in one. Advantages are that it's cheaper than buying two separate drives and only ties up a single IDE/ATA channel. The main disadvantage is having all your eggs in one basket.

QUICK Q&A

What are the benefits of a high-speed drive?

Well, you can install software programs and burn your own CDs more quickly in a fast drive. But that's about it. The fact is that optical drive speeds have reached a practical plateau. We would suggest that you spend more time considering features like buffer under-run protection (stops your drive churning out endless, useless coasters), MultiRead capability (see main section) and even bundled software programs (a DVD movie player and CD burning program are both essential) than speed ratings alone.

Buffer under-run protection (or burn-proofing) is built into most CD and DVD writers these days, and dramatically reduces the number of spoilt discs they churn out. Ordinarily, a drive will spit out an incomplete, useless disc if the flow of data from the hard disk dries up or slows down for even a second, but a buffer gives it some breathing space. The drive may even be able to pause its duties and resume seamlessly when the data stream returns.

PART 2 Other possibilities

There's no shortage of potential add-ons and optional extras for a fledgling computer. Here we discuss a few essentials and suggest some other possibilities.

Modem

An obvious must-have for internet access. You can get internal expansion cards but we would suggest that an external USB model is worth the small additional cost.

The current standard for analogue dial-up modems – i.e. modems that use a standard telephone line to connect to the internet – is V.92, the successor to V.90. While not actually any faster, the V.92 standard includes a 'modem-on-hold' feature that lets you accept a phone call on the same telephone line without dropping a live internet connection. This, however, only works if your Internet Service Provider actively supports modem-on-hold; a V.92 modem alone is not sufficient.

DSL and cable modems are not really modems at all, but that's what you need for broadband internet access. Well, that and a broadband service provider.

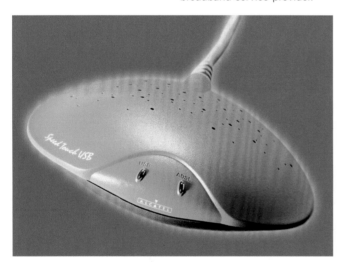

A DSL or cable modem will generally be supplied as part of any broadband internet service deal you sign up to.

Network Interface Card (NIC)

It often makes sense to link computers together in a Local Area Network (LAN). This lets you easily exchange files, share an internet connection and remotely access devices like printers and drives. At its simplest, you can connect two PCs by installing an NIC in each and connecting them with a 'crossover' Category 5 Ethernet cable. To network three or more computers, you need standard non-crossover Category 5 cables with a network hub or switch between them to act as traffic-master. Windows has all the software you need, so network configuration is virtually automatic.

When shopping for an NIC, your main choice is between a card that supports Ethernet (or 10BASE-T) or Fast Ethernet (100BASE-T), or both. These operate with maximum data transfer rates of 10Mbps and 100Mbps respectively. There's also Gigabit Ethernet (1000BASE-T), which is ten times faster than Fast Ethernet, but that's a clear case of overkill in a domestic environment. Dual-speed 10/100 Mbps (Ethernet/Fast Ethernet) internal NIC cards are commonplace, cheap and ideal.

Many motherboards are now natively network-ready, where the Ethernet interface is supported directly by the chipset and an RJ-45 socket is provided on the I/O panel (as in the example on p.22).

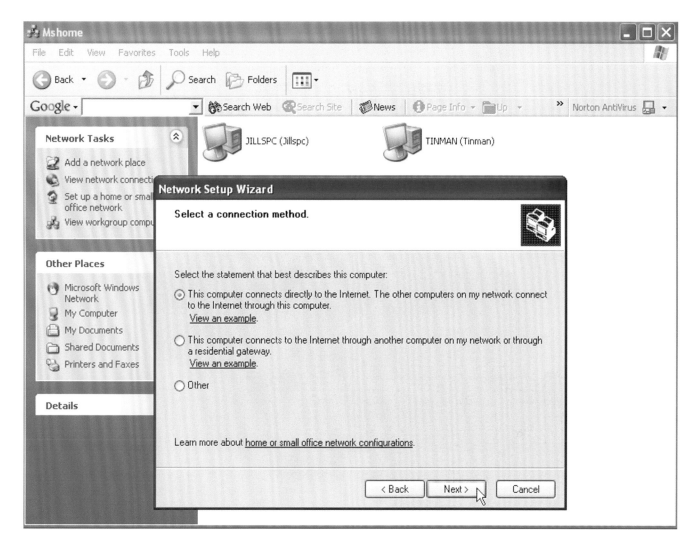

Networking made simple with a
Windows wizard.

FireWire (also known as IEEE-1394 or i.Link)

FireWire is a high-speed (50MB/sec) interface particularly suited
to transferring digital video from camcorder to computer or for
connecting fast external drives. The interface is not usually
provided by the motherboard so you probably need to install a
PCI expansion card to bring FireWire to your computer. However,
the USB 2.0 interface is even faster than FireWire (60MB/sec),
and supported by just about every chipset, so you may find that
you can live without FireWire altogether. Alternatively, choose a
sound card or video card that sports a FireWire port.

It's an Apple trademark but
FireWire works just as well on a
PC as a Mac – if you find a way
to get the interface on-board.

And the rest ...

A mouse, keyboard and monitor are definite givens, and a printer and scanner are obvious peripherals. But how else might you augment your PC?

Headphones and microphone Listen to music or games and record your own voice – or anything else – with a microphone. Windows has a sound recorder built in, but your sound card's software is likely to be more advanced. For use with speech recognition software, the best bet is a quality headset with an earpiece and microphone combined.

Joystick Or other games controller. These usually connect through the MIDI/games or USB port, but you can also get cordless models for greater flexibility.

Games controllers come in all shapes and sizes, from a simple joystick to this (whatever it may be).

Memory card reader A convenient device for transferring files from a memory card of the type used in digital cameras, PDAs, MP3 players and the like. Be sure to get one that's compatible with the type of memory card(s) you use: CompactFlash, SmartMedia, Memory Stick, etc.

PDA and digicam owners might appreciate the convenience of a memory card reader.

TECHIE CORNER

CNR (Communications and Networking Riser) and **AMR** (Audio Modem Riser) are two optional extra slots found on some motherboards. The idea is that a computer manufacturer can integrate modem, sound, USB, networking and other features within a single expansion card, thereby cutting costs. However, CNR and AMR cards are hard to get hold of outside the OEM market, and such motherboard slots are frankly of little interest to the DIY system builder.

USB hub Need more USB ports? A hub can add four or more with ease. You can get standalone external boxes or drive-mounted hubs that provide extra ports on the front of your computer.

IDE controller card Add extra channels to your motherboard and connect another couple of hard disk drives. Essential for RAID, desirable for massive data storage, and of little purpose otherwise.

UPS (Uninterruptible Power Supply) Protect your files from power cuts with a UPS. Basically, it's a mini-generator that kicks in when the lights go out.

If the lights go out unexpectedly, will your data go with them? Not if you invest in a UPS.

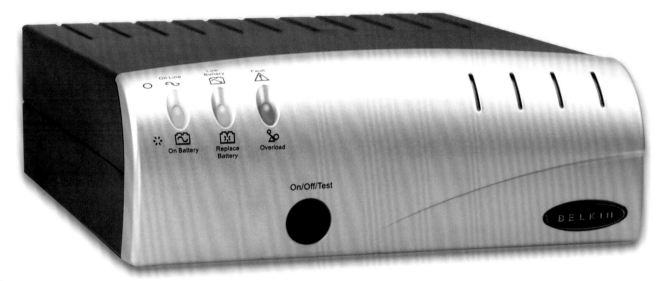

Wi-Fi network If you would like to connect PCs in different rooms but don't particularly fancy running cables around your home, consider a Wi-Fi network. Also known as IEEE 802.11b and wireless Ethernet, this networking technology runs at a maximum speed of 11Mbps in the 2.4GHz radio spectrum. Each computer requires an external USB Wi-Fi adapter or an internal PCI expansion card with a Wi-Fi adapter built-in.

A Wi-Fi adapter gets computers connected at high speeds through the ether.

Webcam 'Stream' live video images across the internet.

Bluetooth A Bluetooth adapter lets your computer 'talk' to and exchange files with other Bluetooth-enabled devices, notably mobile phones and PDAs, without wires.

PART

Summary

A quick review might be in order at this point before we take up tools.

Making choices

The basic decision-making process looks like this:

- **Pick your processor** A Pentium 4 or Athlon XP packs a lot of power; a Celeron or Duron is a good compromise if you don't intend to stretch your hardware.
- **Choose your memory** DDR-RAM or RD-RAM? Sorry Rambus, but we come down firmly in favour of DDR.
- **Integrated multimedia** Decide whether you want on-board sound and video or separate expansion cards.
- **Form factor** ATX and a tower case will likely do nicely.

With these issues settled, you need to find a good motherboard with a chipset that provides all the right features. Sounds simple? Well, it is, more or less. The main factors to consider, check and check again are:

- **Processor support** What socket does the motherboard have? What processor clock speeds does it support? What is the top FSB?
- **Memory support** What type and speed of memory does the motherboard support? Is Dual DDR an option? How much memory can you install? Are there any important restrictions?
- **Multimedia** What AGP speed is supported? If the motherboard has an integrated video chip, is there also a vacant AGP slot? If the motherboard has an integrated sound chip, does it offer surround sound?
- **Hard disk drive support** Does the motherboard provide IDE/ATA, Serial ATA or SCSI channels? What is the maximum bandwidth of the interface?
- **Inputs and outputs** How many PCI expansion slots does the motherboard provide? How many external interfaces/ports are included – and which ones?

A worked example

For this project, we decided to build a mid-range general-purpose Pentium 4-based computer with stacks of expandability. We could as easily have opted for an Athlon XP but the coin came down heads-side up. We also plumped for DDR-RAM because it's cheaper and more readily available than RD-RAM. Integrated sound would be fine but we didn't want an on-board video chip.

   We eventually settled upon an Intel 845 chipset and a Gigabyte GA-8PE667 motherboard. This is by no means an endorsement of one company's products over any other, incidentally, but merely a reflection that you have to buy something eventually!

Here is the full specification:

Feature	Specification	Notes
Form factor	Full-size ATX (305mm x 244mm)	Anything smaller would have fewer features and expansion options.
Chipset	Intel 845PE	See the important notes below about chipset variations.
Processor interface	Socket 478 for Pentium 4	This motherboard supports the 3.06GHz P4 processor, Intel's fastest chip at the time. More than this we obviously could not expect. The alternative would be a Socket A (a.k.a. Socket 472) motherboard if we were going to use an Athlon XP processor.
FSB	533/400MHz	Older P4s ran at 400MHz but the newer versions run at 533MHz. This motherboard supports both speeds. It does no harm to install a 533MHz processor in a 400MHz motherboard but you won't see its full potential.
Memory interface	3 x DDR 184-pin DIMMs	A fourth slot would have been welcome.
Memory bus	266/333MHz	This tells us that the DIMM slots work with either 266MHz or 333MHz memory modules. It would be a shame not to utilise the bandwidth to the full.
Maximum memory	2GB	Windows actually supports up to 4GB of memory so this could be a future limitation. However, we have yet to see any software application stretch a system kitted-out with even a single Gigabyte of RAM so we won't worry too much about this.
Video interface	AGP 4x slot	No integrated video here. Instead, we get a fast four-speed AGP slot. It's not quite cutting edge – we'd need a chipset with 8x AGP support for that – but we're not trying to build a games machine.
Sound chip	Realtek AC '97	Integrated 6-channel audio. We will in fact disable this later and install a PCI expansion card.
Sound ports	Line-out, line-in, microphone-in, MIDI/game port and SPDIF (on expansion bracket)	The standard ports are all incorporated within the main I/O panel. SPDIF is a useful extra that sends a digital multi-channel audio signal to an external device (a recording deck or mixer, perhaps, or a home stereo system).
Expansion slots	6 x PCI	A full complement of six PCI slots is very welcome.
HDD interface	2 x IDE adapters (ATA-33/66/100)	A standard dual-channel configuration that allows us to connect up to four drives, two per channel. We wouldn't have settled for less than an ATA-100 interface, although Serial-ATA would have offered better future-proofing.
Floppy controller	Supports 1.44MB and 2.88MB drives	A motherboard connection for one or two floppy drives.
Inputs/outputs	1 x parallel port, 2 x serial ports, 2 x PS/2 ports	Again, all standard – and, thanks to the prevalence of USB devices, all quite possibly redundant in the near future.
USB	6 x USB 2.0 ports	The chipset supports six USB ports but only two are provided in the main I/O panel. The extra four are installed via an optional bracket connected to the motherboard. Support for the faster USB 2.0 standard rather than old, slow USB 1.1 is essential.
LAN	10/100 Ethernet	A valuable addition. Integrated LAN support means we can hook up our computer to others in a network without having to install an expansion card first.
Modem	Not included	Oh well, we'll just have to buy one. Internal modems use the PCI interface but external USB models are more convenient.
BIOS	Dual BIOS (Award)	Unusually, this motherboard has two BIOS chips to allow for emergency recovery in the event of disaster. We'll cover BIOS in some detail later.

Chipset choices

You have to be careful about precisely which version of a chipset is implemented in your motherboard; don't be swayed by 'Features Intel 845 chipset!' alone. For instance, the chipset we opted for is available in several different flavours:

	845PE	845GE	845G	845E	845GV	845GL	845
FSB (MHz)	533/400	533/400	533/400	533/400	533/400	400	400
Memory support/bus speed (MHz)	DDR/333	DDR /333	DDR/266	DDR/266	DDR/266	DDR/266	DDR/266
Integrated video	No	Yes	Yes	No	Yes	Yes	No
AGP slot	Yes	Yes	Yes	Yes	No	No	Yes

The 845PE is the only chipset here that supports the 533MHz processor bus, the 333MHz DDR-RAM bus and has an AGP slot with no integrated video chip. The relatively humble 845 would be fine were we using an older 400MHz Pentium 4 2.2GHz processor; and the 845GE would be ideal if we wanted fast processor and memory support but also the convenience of integrated video (without sacrificing that important AGP slot).

Our only reservations would be the lack of a Serial ATA HDD interface and the 2GB memory limitation. We might also bemoan the lack of an IEEE-1394 (FireWire) interface, which is particularly useful for connecting a digital camcorder.

RTMM

Read The Motherboard Manual. When we did, two important factors not evident from the spec alone came to light, namely:

- The Intel 845 chipset (and the 850, for that matter) does not provide backward compatibility with 3.3V AGP 2x cards. Although you can physically install such a card, it will do serious damage to the motherboard. Instead, you must install only a 1.5V AGP 4x card or a dual 2x/4x card with jumpers that can be configured to make it operate at 1.5V.

- Although the motherboard supports up to 2GB of RAM across three DIMM slots, you have to follow certain rules when installing the memory modules. In particular, the motherboard – or rather the chipset – only supports four memory banks. A single-sided DIMM has one bank and a double-sided module has two. Thus, if you were to install a double-sided 256MB module in each of DIMM 1 and DIMM 2, the third slot would effectively be redundant. This means that your computer would have 512MB of RAM with no way to add any more short of disposing of an existing, perfectly good module. Moreover, because high-capacity modules are almost always double-sided, the only realistic way to install the maximum possible amount of memory would be to use two (very, very expensive) double-sided 1,024MB modules installed in DIMMs 1 and 2. Alternatively, you might install a double-sided 512MB module in DIMM 1 and two single-sided 256MB modules in DIMMs 2 and 3, thereby reaching a total of 1,024MB. In fact, many permutations are possible but the point is that you must plan carefully and not buy memory on a whim.

The moral of which is ...

Buy your motherboard and read the manual thoroughly before shopping for other key components! You might even download the manual before making a purchase, particularly if you intend to reuse salvaged components and need to rule out incompatibilities. There's nothing worse than having a heap of useless hardware on your hands for want of checking the specs – and yes, that comment is born of bitter experience.

In fact, precisely because of such hidden but critical details, we strongly suggest that you split your component shopping into two stages, punctuated with a bout of manual reading:

1. Buy your motherboard, processor, case and PSU.
2. Buy your memory modules and everything else.

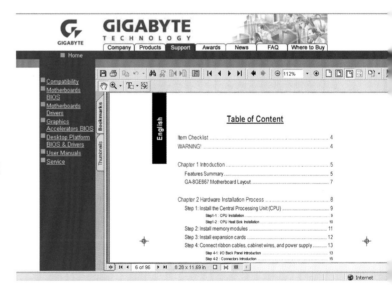

You might be surprised to learn that you can download motherboard manuals from many manufacturers' websites. This is well worth doing before you commit yourself to a particular computer configuration.

A sample shopping list

Finally, here is the full complement of components that we use in the forthcoming project. Your specs and suppliers may well be very different, but it's a useful reference point nonetheless:

Component	Manufacturer	Model/specifications	Notes
Motherboard	Gigabyte	GA-8PE667	As opposite.
Processor	Intel	Pentium 4 2.4B (533MHz FSB, Northwood architecture)	The retail version that comes with a compatible heatsink/fan unit in the box.
Case	Lian-Li	PC-50 aluminium mid-tower ATX	Three 5.25-inch drive bays and three 3.25-inch bays (one hidden).
PSU	Enermax	EG365P 350W	This PSU has the required ATX 12V and ATX Auxiliary connectors.
Memory	Crucial Technology	One 512MB 333MHz DDR-RAM module	Given memory installation restrictions, a single high-capacity module is a better bet than two low-capacity modules.
Hard disk drive	Maxtor	80GB IDE/ATA-100	Fast interface and stacks of storage but Maxtor keeps quiet about the sustained transfer rate.
Floppy disk drive	Teac	1.44MB	It's a floppy drive. What more can we say?
CD-RW drive	Plextor	PlexWriter 48/24/48A	A fast drive with buffer under-run protection, MultiRead compatibility and support for digital audio extraction (pXXX).
DVD-ROM drive	LG Electronics	DRD-8160B	A fast16x/48x-speed MultiRead DVD/CD drive with a software DVD movie player.
Sound card	Creative Labs	Audigy 2 Platinum	6.1 audio, supports EAX, Dolby Digital, THX and DVD Audio, and comes with a drive-mounted breakout box. Also has a FireWire port on the card.
Video card	Creative Labs	3D Blaster® 4 Titanium 4200	A powerful Nvidia-powered AGP 8x card (slight overkill on our AGP 4x motherboard) with DVI support.
Monitor	Iiyama	AS4315UT	17-inch digital TFT monitor.
External USB modem, 5.1 speaker system, PS/2 mouse and PS/2 keyboard	Various	Various	Just some bits and bobs to complete the picture.

3

PART 3 **Putting it all together**

Now comes the time to actually assemble your computer. Start early and you could have a new PC up and running by dinner time. However, you may prefer to start and stop at strategic intervals, so here we break the construction process down into sensible sessions.

PART 3 All set?

Just time for a couple of last-minute checklists

Tooling up

There's no need to equip a workshop with expensive gadgets to build a computer. Here is a full and comprehensive list of all you will need.

- **Antistatic mat and wrist-strap** Electrostatic discharge (ESD) can do serious damage to motherboards and expansion cards, so protect your investment. At a minimum, we strongly recommend that you wear an antistatic wrist-strap whenever handling components. This should be clipped onto an unpainted bare metal part of the computer case. Better still, use an antistatic mat as well. In this case, you connect the wrist-strap cable to the mat and then connect the mat itself to the case. A component should be left safely ensconced within the antistatic bag it came in until you are ready to use it, and then rested on the antistatic mat before installation. Always – and we mean always! – unplug the power cable from the computer before commencing work.

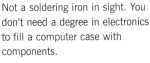

Not a soldering iron in sight. You don't need a degree in electronics to fill a computer case with components.

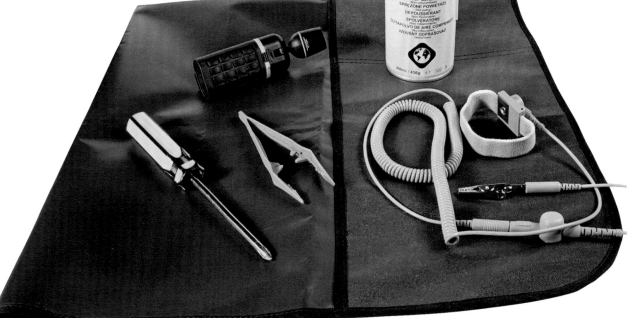

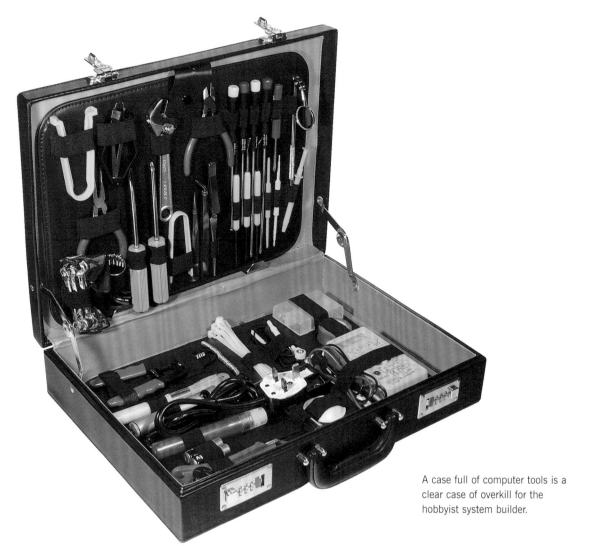

A case full of computer tools is a clear case of overkill for the hobbyist system builder.

- **Screwdrivers** A couple of Phillips and flat-head screwdrivers will suffice.
- **Pliers** Get hold of a pair of plastic pointy pliers or other pick-up implement for setting jumpers and retrieving dropped screws.
- **Air duster** A can of compressed air is more of an ongoing maintenance tool than a construction aid, to be honest, but is useful for de-fluffing and un-clogging second-hand components.
- **Adequate lighting** An Anglepoise or similar light is really useful. Ample daylight is a bonus and a small clip-on torch essential.
- **Patience** Tricky to illustrate on the page but an essential component in any successful PC project. It's best to accept from the outset that not everything will run entirely smoothly. We can guarantee that you will drop the odd screw inside the case, for instance, and it's a fair bet that you will hesitate when required to insert a memory module or heatsink with rather more force than seems reasonable. There's also a chance that something relatively minor – a forgotten cable here, a wrongly set jumper there, a loose connection anywhere – will set you back awhile and force a bout of fraught troubleshooting. But throughout the entire procedure, stay relaxed and think logically. Short of a hardware failure in a specific component, which is itself easily diagnosed, rest assured that your efforts will be rewarded.

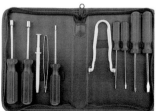

Ready-made screwdriver/pointy-thing kits like this one from Belkin are ideal.

Components

You should now have more or less the following at your disposal:

Hardware
- One case
- One power supply (possibly pre-installed in the case)
- One motherboard
- One processor
- One heatsink with fan
- One or more memory modules
- One hard disk drive
- One floppy disk drive
- One CD-RW drive
- One DVD-ROM drive
- One video card
- One sound card

Peripherals
- One monitor
- One keyboard
- One mouse
- One set of speakers (optional)

Cables, etc.
- Two 80-conductor ATA/IDE cables (one at least should be supplied with the motherboard)
- One floppy drive cable (supplied with the motherboard)
- Audio cable(s) for CD/DVD drives (supplied with the drives)
- Two power cables (one each for the computer and the monitor)
- Drive screws (supplied with the drives)
- Motherboard fixing mounts and screws (supplied with the motherboard)
- Several manuals

Software
- Operating system (probably Windows XP)
- Chipset drivers (supplied with the motherboard)
- Video card/chip drivers (supplied with the video card or motherboard)
- Sound card/chip drivers (supplied with the sound card or motherboard)

Eleven shiny components and one big empty box. Who could resist bringing them together?

CD-RW Drive

DVD-ROM drive

PSU

Motherboard

RAM

Video card

Heatsink/fan

Processor

Floppy disk drvie

Hard disk drvie

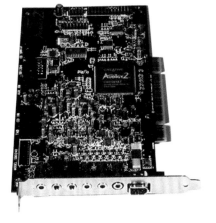
Sound card

Installing a Pentium 4 processor

The first few steps are more easily accomplished before the motherboard is installed in the system case. Set up your antistatic mat on your work surface, touch something metal to discharge any static electricity that you're already carrying, connect and put on your wrist-strap, and carefully remove the motherboard from its protective bag, holding it only by its edges. Now lay it flat on the mat and behold the marvel of microelectronics.

NB If your computer case has a removable motherboard tray, attach the motherboard to it now before going any further. See p.89–90.

Because this is a Pentium 4 motherboard, the processor will be installed in a Socket 478 socket. Note the lever clipped in place along one side of the socket. This is a Zero Insertion Force (ZIF) mechanism that opens the socket's pin holes in preparation for the processor.

Practise first before installing the processor for real. Raise the ZIF lever to the 90° position – you'll feel some slight resistance round about the 65° mark – and then lower it and clip back in place again. Only proceed when you are comfortable with this manoeuvre.

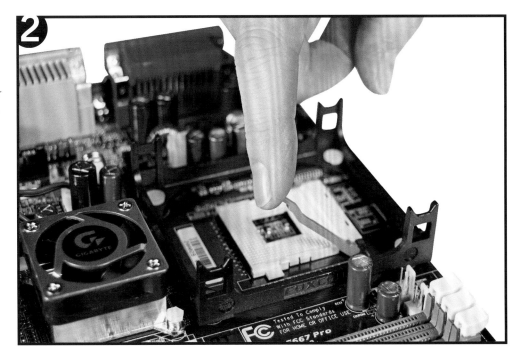

Note the heatsink retention frame, a square plastic contraption fitted around the processor socket. In this example, the motherboard came with the frame pre-installed, but it's possible that you will have to fit it yourself. (The heatsink retention frame is always supplied with the motherboard, incidentally, not the processor.) This is very straightforward: simply snap the frame's four hollow legs into the appropriate pre-drilled holes in the motherboard and secure by pushing plastic pushpins into the legs.

Now raise the socket lever again and remove the processor from its box. Hold it by the edges and be absolutely certain not to (a) touch the pins on its underside or (b) drop it. Your task now is to identify the 'Pin 1' position on both the processor and the socket. On the top of the processor, Pin 1 is clearly indicated by a cutaway corner; on the pin-side, look for a tiny gold triangle and a pair of missing pins.

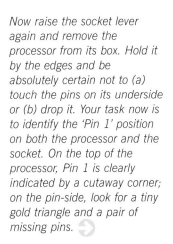

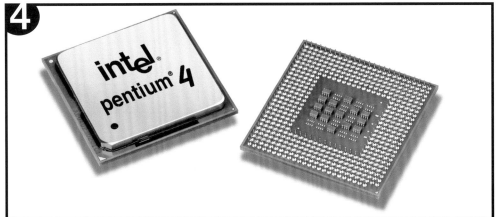

On the socket, Pin 1 is the corner adjacent to the ZIF lever's pivot point. Look closely and you'll see that two pinholes appear to be missing here. These obviously correspond to the missing pins on the processor. Carefully align the processor with the socket, matching the Pin I positions.

Holding the processor by the edges, gently and carefully lower it into the open socket. The processor can only be installed in one orientation and its pins should slip neatly into the socket. The slightest pressure may be required to push it fully home but anything more would indicate that the pins are not properly aligned – in which case, withdraw at once and try again.

When you are certain that the processor is fully engaged – get in close and check this from all angles; it must be completely flush with the socket – lower and clip the ZIF lever. This holds the processor securely into place.

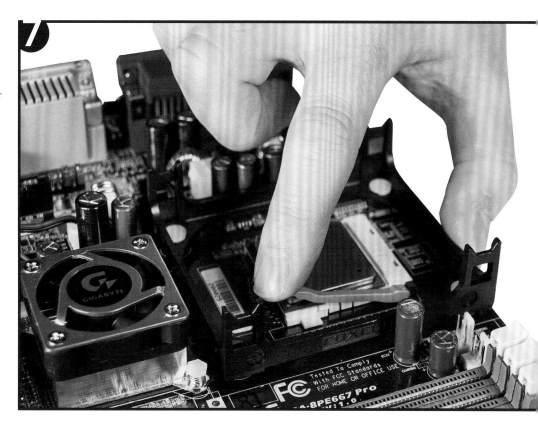

The finished article. The processor is now fully installed in the motherboard socket, where it will perform its duties forever ... or at least until it's time for an upgrade.

Installing a Pentium 4 heatsink

As we discussed earlier, processors require significant cooling. This requires the installation of a heatsink to dissipate heat from the chip.

Our boxed Pentium 4 processor was supplied with an Intel-designed heatsink that has a fan built in. Its successful operation depends entirely upon a good contact being made between the base of the heatsink and the processor, which requires highly-conductive 'thermal interface material' of some description. In this case, a thermal pad has been pre-applied to the underside of the unit. Do not touch, smear, fluff-up dribble on or otherwise interfere with this material. It's possible that you'll have to apply a tube of thermal grease instead, in which case smear it all over the heatsink base as directed.

TECHIE CORNER

Slot-based processor The procedure for installing an old slot-based processor and heatsink is similarly straightforward. Essentially, the processor is encased within a cartridge that fits in a slot on the motherboard, much like an expansion card. Upright plastic stands hold the cartridge in place and the heatsink attaches to one side.

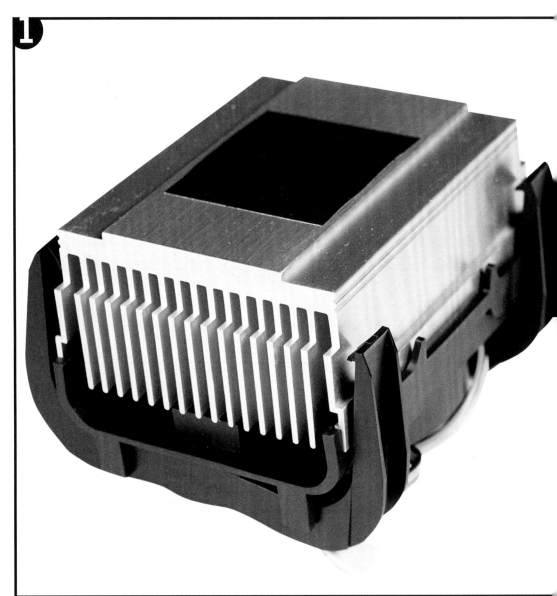

Installation is very simple but try to get it right first time to minimise the risk of disturbing the thermal pad or grease. Position the heatsink above the retention frame and align its four legs with the frame's corner pillars. A simple clip mechanism is designed to secure the heatsink to the retention frame.

Now carefully lower the heatsink onto the frame, ensuring that all four corners are correctly aligned. Press down firmly with both hands. The heatsink will snap into place.

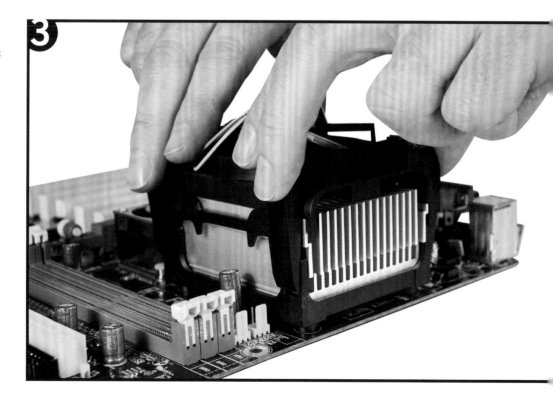

With the heatsink in situ, your next task is to secure it there by means of the two levers on the top of the unit. Hold the unit firmly in place with one hand and slowly, steadily flip one lever through a 180° arc until it locks in place. You may find that this requires a good deal of effort, but don't panic. Now swap hands and repeat with the second lever.

At this point, it's very important to connect the heatsink fan cable to the correct power supply on the motherboard. If you leave this until later and forget, you run the risk of frying both the processor and the motherboard. Dig out your motherboard manual at this point, locate a three-pin socket labelled CPU FAN or PROCESSOR FAN (or similar) on the schematic diagram, and then find this on your actual motherboard. It should be located close to the processor socket. The plug and socket are specially shaped, or keyed, to ensure that the cable cannot be incorrectly connected.

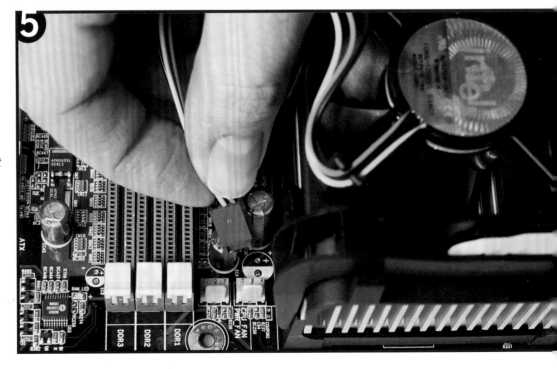

PART 3

Installing an Athlon XP processor

We'll now repeat the previous steps using an Athlon XP processor and heatsink. This is really the only significant practical point of difference between building an Intel- or an AMD-based system. In this example we are going to reuse a heatsink salvaged from a second-hand PC.

When you remove a used heatsink from a motherboard, you will find the remnants of the original thermal material on its base. It is vital to remove this residue thoroughly before reusing the unit. This means attacking it (gently, mind) with a plastic scraper – a credit card, or similar, works just fine.

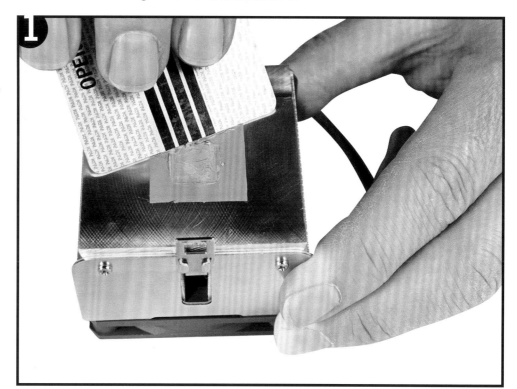

You'll also need some cotton wool and a 'general-purpose fast-drying solvent cleaner to remove any residue' (AMD's words). You should end up with a sparkling, non-greasy aluminium surface on which to attach a new thermal pad.

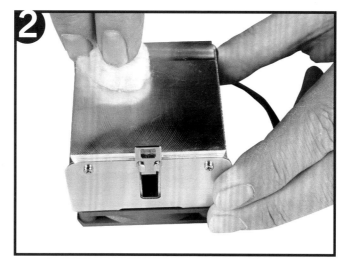

Thermal pads generally come on strips. Remove a single pad, peel off the plastic backing and align it sticky-side down in the middle of the raised section of the heatsink base. Now press down firmly and rub it all over. If you're not happy with the positioning, a misaligned pad is easy to remove at this stage so scrape it off and try again.

Unfortunately, the old processor will also be left with some old thermal gunk that must be removed if you intend to reuse it in a new motherboard. Again, use a cotton bud and solvent and be very, very gentle. The processor die – i.e. the raised silver central section – is the bit to concentrate on here. Use a plastic scraper to remove any excess thermal residue clinging to the edge of the die.

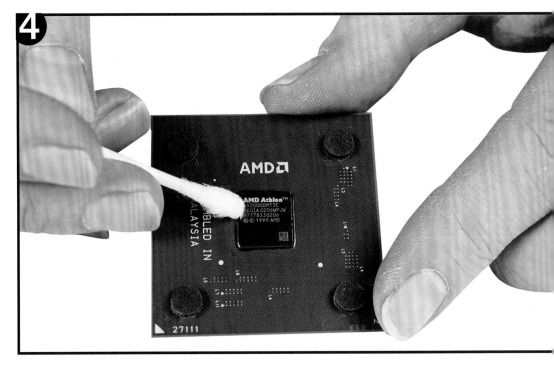

Like the P4/Socket 478 setup we've already seen, the Athlon processor/Socket A arrangement uses Pin 1 positions to ensure that the processor is correctly installed. Look for a small gold triangle stamped on one corner of the processor, both top and pin-side. Pin 1 on the socket is adjacent to the lever's hinge, just like the Socket 478.

To install the processor, raise the socket lever to 90°, pop the processor in the socket – matching the Pin 1 positions – and lower and secure the lever. It's virtually identical to the P4 installation described on p.74–77. Installing the heatsink, however, is another matter entirely.

PART 3 Installing an Athlon XP heatsink

A Socket. A motherboard has no external frame on which to hang a heatsink. Instead, the heatsink must be clipped to the socket itself. Now, we should warn you about two factors at this juncture. First, if you attempt to install the heatsink at an angle (as, to be fair, seems natural), you run a risk of cracking the processor die. Second, while the installation procedure is perfectly straightforward when you've done it a couple of times, first time around you'll swear that the motherboard will shatter if you press any harder in your attempts to clip the heatsink in place. For these reasons, we suggest that you try a dummy run first and install and uninstall the heatsink before the processor is in place.

The base of the heatsink unit has a recessed step that corresponds to a raised lip on the motherboard socket. It also has two side-mounted clips. We'll call the clip adjacent to the recessed step 'clip 1', and the clip opposite 'clip 2'.

TECHIE CORNER

Thermal pads vs. thermal grease
AMD's advice is to use a thermal pad for long-term computer use. The alternative, thermal grease, is fine if you need to remove and replace the heatsink regularly but AMD reckons the grease can dissipate over time. Pentium processors run rather cooler than Athlons and Intel is less concerned about the suitability of thermal grease. Indeed, sometimes it supplies grease in a tube instead of the pre-applied material we saw earlier. If you intend to reuse an Intel heatsink, you can buy a suitable grease from most good computer shops. Always check that it is rated for use with Pentium 4 processors.

Thermal pads or grease help a heatsink dissipate the maximum possible amount of heat away from the hot processor die.

Position the heatsink above the socket and align the recessed step on the heatsink with the socket's raised lip. The trick now is to settle the heatsink onto the socket while simultaneously engaging clip 2 with the plastic tab on the corresponding edge of the socket.

If the clip and tab do not fully engage at the first attempt, press down lightly on the clip with a finger or screwdriver and persuade it into position. Eventually (well, it took us several dummy runs but you may be luckier) the clip should grab the tab and lock in place.

DO NOT tilt the heatsink towards the tab, tempting though it may be. If you do, you will probably crack the processor – an expensive mistake indeed. This is why a practice run pays dividends.

With clip 2 engaged, the recessed step should now be resting on the socket lip with clip 1 positioned directly above the corresponding tab. All that remains is to bring them together. Reach for a small flat-head screwdriver.

The trick here is to hold the heatsink steady – very steady – with one hand while engaging the head of the screwdriver in clip 1. Now press firmly downwards and slightly away from the heatsink until you can hook the clip over and onto the retaining tab. Yes, it really does take a good deal of force. Eventually, you'll hear a satisfying click as the clip and tab lock horns.

Make absolutely certain that both clips are FULLY engaged with their respective tabs; the last thing you need is for an imperfectly attached heatsink to fall off the motherboard during operation. To release the heatsink, hold the unit steady again, re-engage the screwdriver in clip 1 and push down and away from the heatsink until the clip springs free from the retention tab. Clip 2 can now be teased away from its tab and the entire heatsink removed.

All that remains is to repeat the installation procedure with the processor in place. Remember to remove the backing paper from the thermal pad on the base of the heatsink first and connect the heatsink's power cable to the appropriate socket on the motherboard as soon as it's in place.

Once contact has been made between the pad and the processor, it is vital that the bond is nor disturbed. If you have to abort the procedure during the hard part – Step 6 above – clean the heatsink and processor, replace the thermal pad and start again.

Installing RAM

One other job that can be accomplished now is installing your memory modules. First consult your motherboard manual for directions. Here, the motherboard supports a maximum of either two double-sided modules or one double-sided module plus two single-sided modules (p.66).

If using Rambus memory, you must fill all unused memory slots with dummy modules known as Continuity RIMMs, or CRIMMs. Again, your motherboard manual will make this clear.

In this worked example, we will install a single 184-pin 512MB module of DDR RAM in DIMM 1, leaving the other two DIMMS free for future upgrades.

1 — *DIMM slots should be numbered on the motherboard but can otherwise be identified with the help of a schematic diagram in the motherboard manual. At each end of the slot are plastic clips. Flip these open on your first DIMM by pushing down and away from the slot. Now remove the memory module from its antistatic bag, holding it only by the ends to avoid contact with the memory chips or the lower connecting edge. Align it carefully with the DIMM slot. The module and slot are both keyed with notches to ensure the correct orientation.*

2 — *Push down on the module with your thumbs until the plastic clips snap shut and secure the module in place. Again, you may be surprised or nervous about how much pressure you have to apply to coax the module into its new home. But take it easy, be sure that you keep the module vertical, and double-check that it is correctly aligned with the slot. Repeat with other modules as required.*

PART **3**

Installing the motherboard

Your motherboard is now host to a processor, a heatsink and some memory. Unfortunately, that's about as far as we can go with the motherboard perched so conveniently on our antistatic mat. Now we need to install it in the case.

If your computer case has a removable tray, you should attach the motherboard to it before installing any other components. Just follow the steps below. The advantage of the tray mechanism is that you don't have to fiddle with screws and standoffs inside the case.

Which is precisely what we'll do now with our tray-less case. Always work with the case on its side so the motherboard goes in flat, and exercise caution: you wouldn't be the first to behead a capacitor with a slippery screwdriver. If your case has a power supply pre-installed, you may find that it partially blocks access to the motherboard. Reverse the procedure discussed on p.91–92 to remove it for the meantime.

QUICK Q&A

My motherboard doesn't fit!
Actually, it does – unless, of course, you have made the mistake of obtaining an incompatible form factor. Industry standards guarantee that any ATX motherboard will fit any ATX case. However, this is not quite the same as saying that it will fit without a fiddle. You may find that the first couple of screws go in just fine but then the other holes appear to be slightly out of alignment. Motherboards are not inherently flexible but we have yet to be beaten by one, even when it took a measure of pushing and pulling and even a second pair of hands.

A removable tray makes it very much easier to fit the motherboard. The tray is then screwed back into place inside the case with the motherboard, processor and memory all on-board.

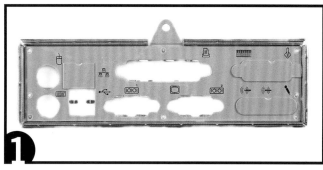

1

Your motherboard will be supplied with an I/O (input/output) shield. This lets various ports poke through designated holes in the rear of the case. Now, manufacturers have some latitude over where they place these ports and some motherboards have more than others. If your case already has a shield fitted, compare it to the shield supplied with your motherboard. If they are absolutely identical – i.e. have all the same holes in exactly the same places – leave well alone: your motherboard will fit just fine. If not, snap out the case shield and snap in the new one.

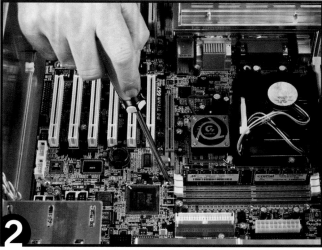

2

A motherboard is typically installed by screwing it to raised brass or plastic standoffs that must first be attached to the case or tray. You will find many more fittings for the standoffs than you actually need because the case has been designed to accept a variety of motherboard sizes, including scaled-down ATX form factors. To determine where your standoffs should go, hold the motherboard in place within the case or on tray. Align its I/O panel with the I/O shield and match the motherboard's pre-drilled holes with the standoff positions. Now attach the standoffs as per the case instructions and screw the motherboard into place. DO NOT overtighten the screws as that risks cracking the motherboard. Should you drop a screw (you will, we promise), retrieve it with your trusty plastic pliers.

TECHIE CORNER

Jumpers An older motherboard with, say, a Socket 7 socket for a Pentium processor is likely to have a set of hardware jumpers that must be set correctly. These jumpers – little plastic shunts attached to tiny pins, similar to the jumpers on a drive (see p.99) – control essential elements of motherboard operation, including the bus speed and the processor type and voltage. However, most modern motherboards have evolved beyond jumpers and control this sort of business by means of the BIOS.

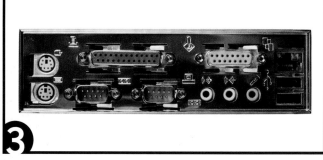

3

Take care that the motherboard's I/O panel perfectly matches the I/O shield in the case, with no ports obscured or blocked. As mentioned above, take great care with your screwdriver, too – one slip-up here and you could easily trash the motherboard. If using a tray, attach this to the case now as per the instructions.

PART 3

Installing the PSU

If your case came with a PSU pre-installed and you were able to install the motherboard without first removing it, well and good. In this project, however, the PSU was a separate acquisition.

Standard 3-pin female power cables (technically known as IEC 320 EN 60320 C13, but just ask in Maplin) are all you need for your computer and monitor.

PSUs usually attach by mean of four screws. A PSU unit is a heavy beast, as you will now discover, so you may find a supporting shelf or ledge inside the case. Hold the PSU in position and screw it into place. Do not overtighten the screws but ensure that the PSU has no room for movement.

In our example, it's plain that the PSU partially obscures the motherboard so it would have to be removed before we could uninstall the motherboard or even access key components like the processor. This is one price you pay for a smaller case.

TECHIE CORNER

Old AT-style PSUs We're not covering them here but there's one point that really must be made: older AT-style PSUs have two motherboard connectors that must be plugged into the motherboard side-by-side. They are not keyed so it's perfectly possible to get them the wrong way around — in which case you risk destroying the motherboard. It is absolutely essential that the black wires in each connector are aligned together.

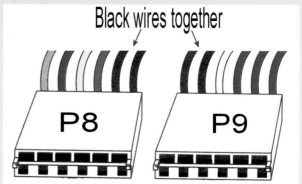

If for reasons best know to yourself you end up with an AT-style motherboard and PSU, be very careful indeed to connect the two plugs to the motherboard with the black wires together.

Cable connections

We will now use the abundance of spaghetti-like cables spewing forth from the PSU to connect it to the motherboard in several different ways. This particular PSU has a 6-pin ATX Auxiliary cable connection (p.42) but the motherboard itself has no use for it. That's fine; we'll just tuck it out of harm's way later. Again, though, we reiterate that if your motherboard has an ATX Auxiliary socket, you must use it. If your PSU doesn't have the requisite cable and plug, it's time to source a new one.

TECHIE CORNER

There is some merit in powering up the computer as it stands at this point. Without a keyboard, video card, monitor or hard disk, you're not going to get very far but you can at least check that the heatsink and case fans are working. You should also see a small light illuminate on the motherboard, which confirms that power is coming through.

Check that the PSU is set to the correct voltage – 220/240V in the UK – and connect it to the mains electricity with a female 3-pin power cable. Now turn the PSU's power switch to the On position and press the On/Off button on the front of the case. You needn't put the case covers on or even sit the case upright at this stage; this is a very simple test that won't take a moment.

As the motherboard powers up, it will emit a series of coded beeps. You can interpret these codes if you have a mind to (p.132) but any beeps at all is a sure sign of life. It also confirms that the case speaker is working. If you hear nothing, check the speaker cable connection.

When you're finished, turn off the computer with the case button, then switch the PSU to Off and unplug the power cable.

QUICK Q&A

This front panel business is too fiddly for words. Can't I connect these cables before the motherboard goes into the case?
Possibly. If your case has a removable motherboard tray, you may find that you can make the front panel cable connections before screwing the tray into the case. If your motherboard attaches directly to the case chassis, however, it is unlikely that the cables will stretch beyond the confines of the case to the motherboard lying on your mat. It's worth a try, though.

First, plug the large 20-pin ATX power connector (usefully labelled MAIN here) into the appropriate socket on the motherboard. This connector is keyed so it only fits one way around. Align it carefully and push fully home.

Now connect the PSU's ATX 12V cable. A clip mechanism ensures that, once fitted, it will not pop out again. At this point you should also connect the ATX Auxiliary cable if the motherboard has a socket (see above). Take a moment to check that the processor fan cable is still securely connected.

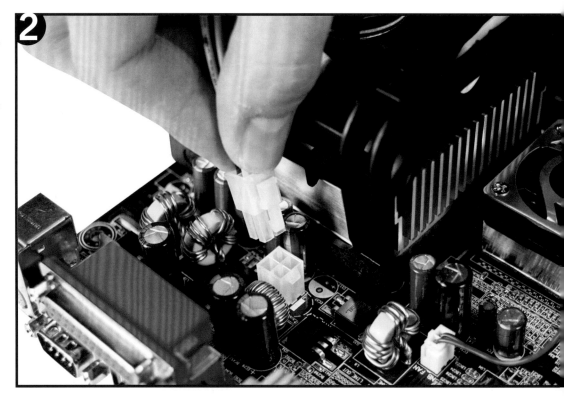

Your computer case will come with one or possibly two fans built-in with cables attached. This case happens to have two: a top-mounted extraction fan and a front-mounted air intake fan. All motherboards have one system fan connector (labelled PWR FAN here) but not all have two. If your case has just one fan, connect it to the 3-pin motherboard socket. Here, the case manufacturer sensibly assumed that the motherboard might not have a second fan socket and so equipped the fan cable with a pass-through adapter that lets it tap into a main drive power cable.

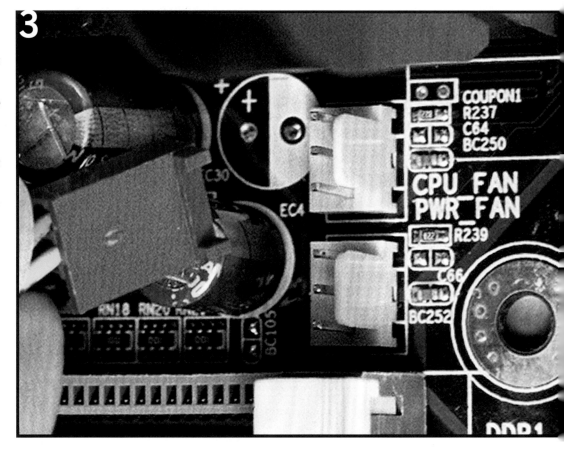

On behalf of the computer industry, please accept our heartfelt apologies at this juncture. It is time to wire-up a bunch of cables with tiny connectors that control various features of the case, including the on/off and reset switches, the case lights and the speaker. Locate the relevant 'front panel' sockets on the motherboard – and take a deep breath.

One day, perhaps, there will be a catch-all connector that makes this a cinch, but for now you have to carefully match fiddly connectors to fiddly sockets with long-nosed plastic pliers and intuition.

The plugs may be named – Speaker, Reset Switch and so forth – and the cables may be colour-coded, but there's no guarantee that the motherboard will use the same descriptions or that the manual will decode the non-standard colour-scheme. None of these mini-plugs are keyed so it's all too easy to get the positive/negative polarity mixed up.

All you can do is use whatever information the case and motherboard manuals supply between them to ascertain as best you can what goes where. Later, if the power and drive activity lights fail to function when you power-up the PC, dive back in here and turn the 2-pin plugs through 180° to reverse the polarity. The power and reset switches will work regardless of polarity.

PART ③ **Installing the floppy disk drive**

We will now install the first of four internal drives. As noted earlier, the floppy disk drive is rapidly approaching extinction, but we still have a soft spot for the old stalwart.

❶ The precise procedure for installing any drive depends upon the specific design of your case. Here, the case fascia must be completely removed to provide access to the drive bays. With some case designs, you can remove a separate drive bay cage, screw the drives into place and then refit the finished cage within the case. Here, however, the drive bays are integral to the chassis.

❷ Inside the case, you will find two or three 3.5-inch drive bays, and possibly a separate cage for a couple more. This case has three. The uppermost drive bay has no corresponding cover so we'll reserve this for the hard disk drive, as it requires no external access. The floppy drive may be sited in either of the remaining bays.

Remove one of the 3.5-inch drive bay covers. It might snap off, slide off, pop out or pop in, but one way or another it can be removed. Now slide the floppy disk drive into the appropriate drive bay (from within or without, whichever is easier). Some drive bays incorporate runners or supports that hold drives in position, but not so here.

Ensure that the front of the drive is flush with the front of the case; or, if your case has a curved or shaped fascia, is set neither too far back to be accessible nor too far forward. Here we replaced the case fascia to find the correct position. Secure in place with four drive screws supplied. DO NOT overtighten these screws: you may damage the drive or at least strip the screw-heads.

Two cable connections must now be made. First, locate the appropriate power cable with a female 4-pin mini-plug that is significantly smaller than all the others (Berg-style). Connect this to the drive's power socket, matching the orientation of plug and socket. Also connect the floppy drive's data cable. This has a twist along its length, which makes it clearly distinguishable from all-flat IDE/ATA ribbon cables. Check any markings on the drive for a clue about which side of the socket is Pin 1, and pair this with the cable's pink stripe.

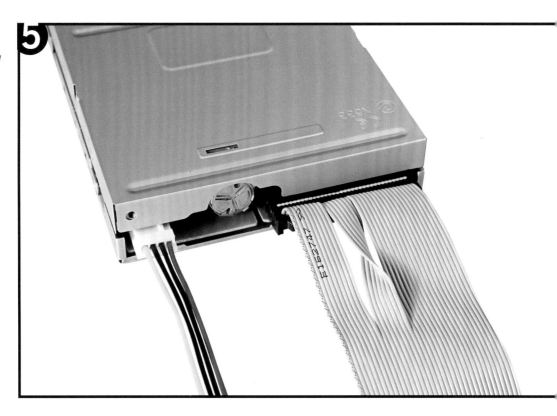

The other end of the data cable now connects to the floppy drive controller socket on the motherboard (there is only one). The plug and socket are keyed to prevent erroneous installation. Push it home firmly. That's it: you now have, or soon will have, a functional floppy disk drive.

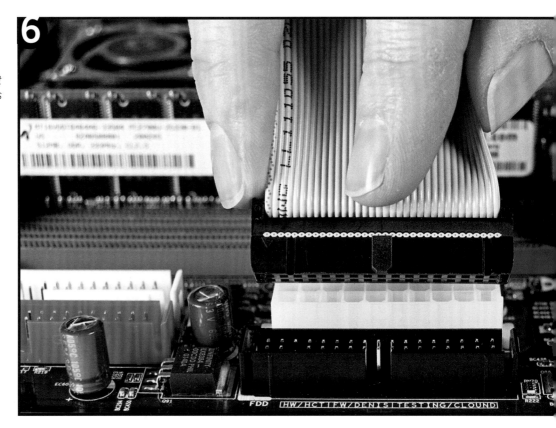

Installing the hard disk drive

This is very similar to the floppy drive procedure but with a couple of extra considerations in the form of jumpers and cable concerns.

QUICK Q&A

How do I work out where the jumper is supposed to go?
The hard disk drive case should have a printed diagram that illustrates all the possible jumper configurations. In our experience, however, some don't. If the drive was supplied with a manual or even a scrap of paper, look to it for instructions; if not, check the manufacturer's website. A company called Ontrack also maintains a very useful online database of drive/jumper details. See Appendix 3 for contact details.

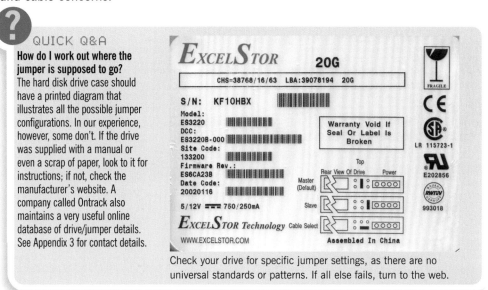

Check your drive for specific jumper settings, as there are no universal standards or patterns. If all else fails, turn to the web.

On the rear of the hard disk drive, you will find sockets for the data and power cables. Alongside these is an array of pins with a plastic shunt, or 'jumper'. This is important because each IDE/ATA channel on the motherboard can control two devices, but one must be designated Master and one Slave. This position of the jumper on the pins determines the drive's status. If you are using an 80-conductor cable, as you should be, the easiest thing is to use the Cable Select jumper position. Alternatively, set the jumpers to Master. Your plastic pliers will prove useful here.

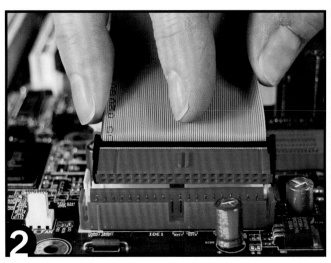

TECHIE CORNER

Anatomy of an IDE/ATA cable A standard 80-conductor has three plugs. One end, usually coloured blue, connects to the motherboard socket. At the opposite end is the Master device plug, usually coloured black. Whichever drive you plug this into is automatically assigned Master status on the ITE/ATA channel (assuming its jumpers are set to Cable Select). The Slave device plug, usually coloured grey, is located about a third of the way along the cable from the Master plug. This colour-coding is malleable, though; in our project, the motherboard manufacturer chose red for the IDE1 channel and supplied a cable that was coloured correspondingly.

Older 40-conductor cables cannot determine the status of a device so it doesn't matter which plug you connect to which drive. The Master/Slave business must be controlled entirely by the drive jumpers.

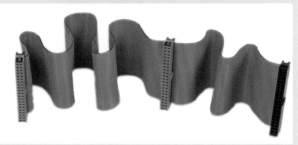

An 80-conductor IDE/ATA has 80 fine wires, three coloured plugs, a red 'Pin I' stripe and a built-in brain (of sorts).

It is sound advice to make the hard disk drive the sole device on the primary IDE/ATA channel (IDE1), so identify this socket on your motherboard now. IDE1 is usually colour-coded blue but here it happens to be red; we know not why. Connect the appropriate plug on the 80-conductor cable (see Techie Corner).

Slide the drive into a 3.5-inch drive bay with no corresponding drive bay opening on the front of the case (the drive must be completely concealed within the case) and screw into place with four drive screws.

Connect the other end of the IDE/ATA cable to the drive. Be careful to match the stripe on the cable with the drive's Pin 1 position. In practice, both plug and socket are keyed to prevent mistakes but Pin 1-to-Pin 1 remains gospel.

Finally, connect the power cable. This time you need one of the larger 4-hole female Molex-style plugs. Again, the plug and socket are shaped to ensure that it is (very nearly) impossible to connect the cable incorrectly.

PART

Installing the CD and DVD drives

Optical drives – CD and DVD in all their fancy flavours – use 5.25-inch drive bays. Our case has three such bays, but yours may have five or six, depending on its height. We will install a CD-RW drive first.

Like the hard disk drive, a CD-RW drive has a set of jumpers on its rear end. Once again, we'll use an 80-conductor cable so the jumper position can be set to Cable Select. If you have only a 40-conductor cable, which is technically sufficient for an optical drive, set the jumpers to Master.

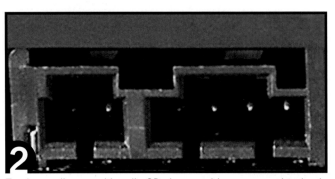

To play audio or multimedia CDs in your drive, you need to hook it up to a sound card or integrated sound chip (but see p.121). Most modern drives have two audio outputs, analogue and digital, and most sound cards have corresponding sockets of both types. Here, we'll connect a 4-pin analogue cable to the CD drive and reserve the 2-pin digital option for the DVD drive. It's much easier to connect this fiddly cable to the drive now before it is installed within the case.

 QUICK Q&A

My IDE/ATA cable isn't long enough to connect my drive(s) to the motherboard!

The maximum recommended length for ribbon IDE/ATA cables is 45cm (18 inches). In a really tall case, this might not be long enough to connect the topmost optical drive. The solution is to buy a longer cable or use lower drive bays. Some degradation in the signal is supposedly possible with long cables but we have never seen this become a practical problem. Using a non-standard cable would be more problematic with the hard disk drive but 3.5-inch drive bays are typically located within easy reach of the motherboard's IDE/ATA sockets.

 TECHIE CORNER

Digital Audio Extraction Thanks to a process known as Digital Audio Extraction, it is often possible to dispense with audio cables altogether. If a drive supports DAE, the sound signal is channelled to the sound card through the IDE/ATA bus instead. If you're unsure whether your drives support DAE, we suggest that you start off by using audio cables and revisit the subject later when you have speakers connected (see p.121).

 QUICK Q&A

Does it matter which drive I make the Master and which the Slave?

No. All that matters from your computer's point of view is that it can tell one channel-sharing drive from the other. The Master/Slave nomenclature is misleading because neither drive actually has priority over the other. If you only install one drive on a channel, as we did with the hard disk, you should of course make it the Master device.

With the jumpers set and the audio cable connected, snap/poke/pull/push off a drive bay cover and slide the device into place. Use one of the uppermost drive bays in a tower case. The position of the plugs on a ribbon cable makes it much easier to connect a second drive to the same cable when it is located below the first.

3

4

Connect the blue plug on an 80-conductor IDE/ATA cable to the secondary IDE controller on the motherboard, and the black plug to the drive. Also connect a power cable. As with the floppy drive, check that the drive is flush with the front of the case before you screw it into place. The audio cable can hang loose inside the case for now, but tuck it away from fans and motherboard components.

5

The DVD drive can now be installed in exactly the same way. This time, however, use a digital audio cable. Set the jumpers to Cable Select (or Slave if using a 40-conductor cable) and secure the drive in the drive bay immediately below the CD drive. Connect the power cable and again ensure that the audio cable can't interfere with anything inside the case.

This drive will share the secondary IDE channel with the CD drive so it must use the grey plug on the same ribbon cable. As ever, the striped edge of the cable must tally with the drive's Pin 1 position.

PART **3**

Installing the video card

Our fledgling PC is coming along very nicely. The motherboard is installed in the case, the processor, heatsink and memory module(s) are all attached, and we've connected floppy disk, hard disk, CD and DVD drives. Next we will install a video card.

Locate the AGP slot on your motherboard – here it happens to be colour-coded purple – and remove the corresponding blanking plate from the case. It may need unscrewing (in which case keep the screw), or it may slide or pop out.

Remove the video card from its protective antistatic packaging. You should still be wearing your antistatic wrist-strap and using an antistatic mat, of course. Be careful not to touch the electrical contacts on the bottom edge – greasy fingerprints are lousy for connectivity – or any of the onboard components. Position the card lightly in the AGP slot, matching any notch on the card with the shape of the slot. Do not apply any pressure just yet.

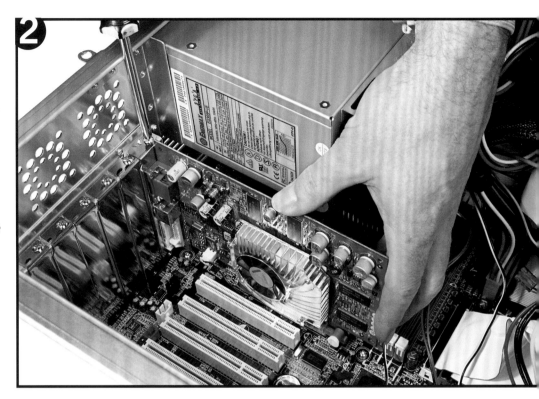

AGP 4x and faster slots incorporate a card retention mechanism. Designs vary but essentially this is here to support and secure the card. Here, we have a pushpin arrangement. Withdraw the pushpin with one hand and press vertically downwards on the card with the other hand until it slides fully home in the slot.

4 When the card is evenly seated in the AGP slot, release the pushpin or otherwise close the card retention mechanism. The card's external faceplate should be neatly aligned with the space in the case. Screw the card to the chassis frame using either the screw you removed earlier or one supplied with the card. As always, refrain from overtightening.

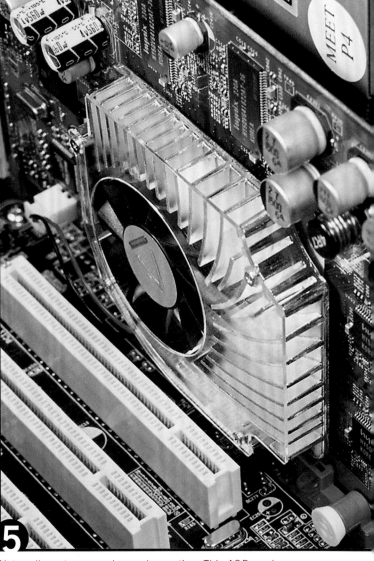

5 Not really a step, merely an observation. This AGP card comes perilously close to overhanging the neighbouring PCI slot. There is still some clearance but installing a card next to it would certainly impede airflow to the video card's heatsink/fan. If you have a port bracket to install, this would be the best PCI slot to sacrifice (see p.120–121).

Integrated video

If you have procured a motherboard with onboard video, you will need to connect the supplied VGA port bracket to the video chip on the motherboard. The bracket will have a cable and plug pre-fitted, so consult the manual and find the right socket on the motherboard. Then remove a blanking plate and screw the bracket into place. This simple procedure gives your computer an external VGA port to which a monitor may be attached.

Should you later wish to upgrade to a standalone video card, you will probably have to disable the onboard video chip. We say probably because some motherboards automatically disable integrated video in favour of an AGP card as soon as one is installed. Alternatively, your motherboard may have a jumper that needs to be reset to disable onboard video. If you use a PCI card, however, you will certainly need to tweak the BIOS settings.

Disabling onboard video is usually done something like this:
- Turn off your computer and install the PCI video card in a free slot.
- As you restart the computer, enter the BIOS Setup program (see p.112). Look for a sub-menu called PnP/PCI configurations, or similar, find an entry called Initial Display, or similar, and enable PCI video as the default option. If these menus are not present, look for an Advanced BIOS Features sub-menu.
- Now save your changes, exit BIOS, turn off your computer and connect the monitor to the new video card.
- Reboot and let Windows install a basic video driver. This will get the card working and produce an image on the screen. You can then install any drivers or application software supplied with the card.

Your video card will 'just work' straight out of the box, but you'll see nothing like its full potential until you install its specialist drivers.

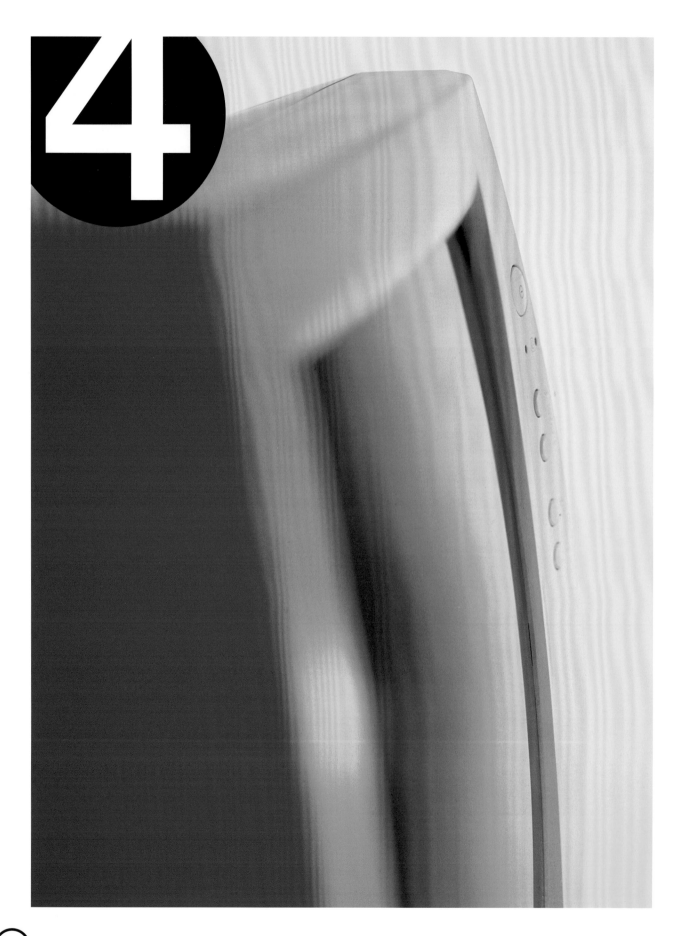

4

PART **4** **Final touches**

We told you it was easy. All that remains now is to set up the computer to behave to your liking, install an operating system and finish off with a final expansion card. We will cover troubleshooting in some detail, too, just in case of problems.

Connecting a monitor and switching on

At this point in the proceedings, you might be tempted to rush into further installations: the sound card, perhaps, or an internal modem or network card. However, now is the time to establish that everything has so far gone according to plan. Adding extra components merely complicates troubleshooting, should any be required.

Before going live, give your computer a thorough internal inspection. It is unusual but not impossible for cables and plugs to work loose, particularly those fiddly ones that power fans and the front panel switches.

Check it out

Give your work-in-progress a thorough once-over. Check that the heatsink and case fans are all still connected to the motherboard, that the memory modules are still clipped into their DIMMS or RIMMS, that the drives are all wired-up with ribbon and power cables, and that the AGP video card is fully secured. You might like to reassemble the case now but it's not strictly necessary. You can even leave the case lying on its side to better monitor the action. However, you will be working with live electricity from here on, so observe the golden rule: never touch anything inside your PC's case while the PSU is connected to the mains power. Even when you turn off your computer, the PSU continues to draw power from the mains and the motherboard remains in a partially-powered standby state. We're only talking a 5V current, to be fair, but it's simply crazy to work on a 'live' motherboard or anything connected to it.

True, you could flip the PSU to Off (if it has its own power switch) and/or turn off the electricity at the wall socket (and hope that Junior doesn't turn it back on for a laugh while your head is buried in the case), but it's better and safer to get into the habit of always removing the power cable before conducting any internal work. This is the only cast-iron way to ensure no physical connection between yourself and the National Grid.

Booting up … and down again

Connect the monitor to the video card's VGA or DVI port and plug it in to the mains with one of your 3-pin IEC-320 cables. Also connect a PS/2-style keyboard (see the Techie Corner box on p.113). Turn on the monitor now. You might see a 'no signal' or similar message on the screen.

Now check that the PSU is set to the correct voltage – 220/240V in the UK – and connect it to the mains with your second power cable. Flip the PSU's power switch to the on position. Finally, press the on/off button on the front of the case. Your PC will come to life for the first time (or second time if you tested it back on p.93).

Look inside the case and check – by observation, not by touch – that the heatsink and case fans are whirring. If not, kill the mains power immediately and check the fan cable connections on the motherboard. Ignore any beeps for now.

All being well, power-down your computer with the on/off button and unplug the power cable. Leave the power switch on the PSU at the on position from now on. If all is not well, skip to p.124 now for some troubleshooting procedures.

Let us now turn our attention to some important configuration settings.

With a keyboard and monitor connected, you can see the power flowing into your creation. Dr Frankenstein must have felt this way.

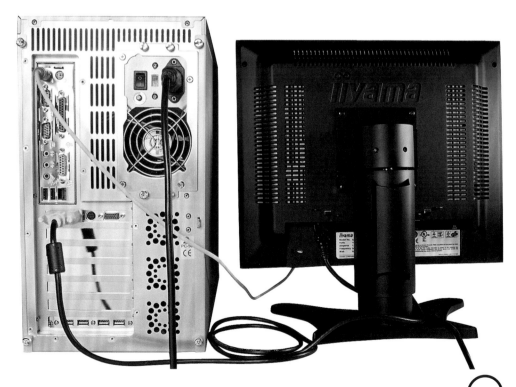

FINAL TOUCHES

PART 4 BIOS setup

When you're used to working in a Windows environment, the text-only world of BIOS menus can seem a little daunting. You can certainly cripple your computer if you make careless changes, so do tread carefully.

CMOS and BIOS

CMOS (Complementary Metal-Oxide Semiconductor) is a special kind of small-scale memory embedded in a chip soldered to the motherboard and powered by a battery. It maintains a record of the date and time, how much memory your PC has and which hardware devices are attached. It is only by reference to CMOS during the power-up procedure that the computer knows it is a computer at all and not, for instance, a peach. Without CMOS, it would have to laboriously re-identify itself every time.

CMOS is not something that need concern you during the everyday operation of your computer but it does require some configuration at the outset. This is handled through the BIOS Setup program.

BIOS ROM (Basic Input/Output System Read-Only Memory) is a separate chip on the motherboard that contains – or, rather,

that is – a set of instructions and drivers intended to get the computer up and running before Windows (or any other operating system) kicks in. BIOS lets you manually configure the information held in CMOS. To access its Setup program, you must press a specific key or combination of keys as the computer is powering up. Your motherboard manual should make this clear but the chances are that it's Delete, Escape, F1 or F2. You may see 'Press DEL to enter SETUP', or a similar message, appear on screen as the computer starts. If you don't see any prompts and the manual draws a blank, repeatedly press the Delete, Escape, F1 or F2 keys as soon as the computer's POST procedure (p.127) completes its memory count.

Reconnect your power cable now, turn on your computer and find your way into BIOS.

Watch the screen closely for clues about how to get into BIOS. Here it is merely a matter of hitting the Delete key at just the right moment.

TECHIE CORNER

Plug-and-Play BIOS A modern Plug-and-Play BIOS will automatically detect and configure a hard disk drive. This is exceedingly useful as it saves you having to manually enter information about cylinders, heads, landing zones, sectors, access modes and the like. This information can be gleaned from the drive's manual, of course, or perhaps from a printed panel on the drive itself, or at least from the manufacturer's website if all else fails. But it's a definite hassle and all too easy to get a setting wrong.

BIOS basics

There are, inevitably, many BIOS programs around. In the following example, we will be working with the Award-made BIOS program used on our Gigabyte motherboard. You should be able to interpret your own motherboard's BIOS in a similar manner, even if it should look rather different.

Working with BIOS is a matter of selecting options on menus, making changes where necessary and then saving these changes to CMOS. The BIOS Setup program should include a guide as to which keyboard keys govern each action; if not, press F1 for help. These are the keys that control our Award BIOS:

Up Arrow	Move to previous item on a menu
Down Arrow	Move to the next item on a menu
Left Arrow	Move to an item to the left of the current position
Right Arrow	Move to an item to the right of the current position
Escape	Quit the current menu
Page Up	Increase the selected item's current numeric value
Page Down	Decrease the selected item's current numeric value
F1	BIOS help
Enter	Confirm a selection
F10	Exit BIOS and save changes

Tweaking BIOS

We are concerned with three settings here. We want to set the date and time, disable the motherboard's onboard audio, and enable the CD-RW drive as a boot device.

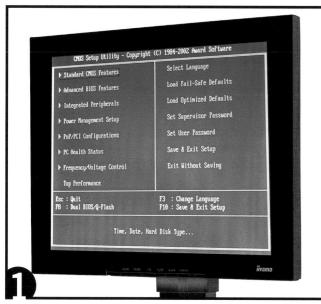

The computer's time and date settings are found within a CMOS sub-menu. Use the up/down/left/right arrow keys to select (highlight) a menu option called Standard CMOS Features – it's at the top of the left-hand column here – and press Enter to access the sub-menu.

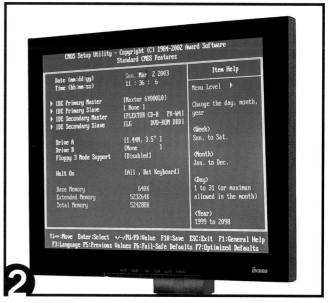

You may find that the date and time are already correct because the motherboard manufacturer pre-set them in the factory. If not, select each entry in turn with the arrow keys and then press Page Up or Page Down to change the value. For instance, if the month entry currently says January but it's really July, select Jan and press the Page Down key repeatedly until Jul appears. Now press Enter to confirm the change and move onto the next entry with the arrow keys. When you're finished, press Escape to return to the main menu page.

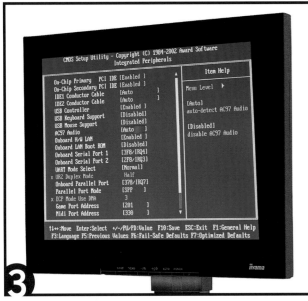

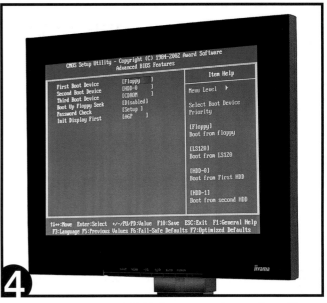

The onboard audio setting is tucked away within the Integrated Peripherals sub-menu. Select that now, press Enter to get to the sub-menu and locate the relevant variable. In this case it is: AC97 Audio [Auto].

Move through the menu with the Down Arrow key until [Auto] is selected, and press Page Down. This changes the value to [Disabled]. Now press Enter to confirm. Finally, press Escape to return to the main menu. Your computer has been rendered mute but is now ready for a sound card.

Next, highlight Advanced BIOS Features and press Enter. Here, we see the order in which the computer looks to its drives as it powers up: floppy disk drive followed by hard disk drive followed by CD-ROM drive. In other words, if the computer finds a floppy disk with a bootable program, it will load and run that program. If not, it moves on to the hard disk. In the normal course of events, here it will find Windows and all will be well with the world. Our hard disk is currently barren, of course, so the computer will continue and check any or all installed optical drives. That's just what we want, as we intend to install Windows directly from a CD (p.116).

Make sure that your CD drive is included in the list of bootable devices. Select the boot device position immediately after the hard disk drive and use the Page Up and Page Down keys to scroll through available devices. Press Enter to add a drive to the list.

QUICK Q&A

What if I don't bother disabling audio before installing a sound card?
Well, everything may well work for the best, with the motherboard BIOS automatically assigning priority to the sound card over the onboard chip. But it may not, in which case conflicts and confusion reign and you may get no audio output at all. You should be able to recover from such a state by physically uninstalling the sound card and removing all its drivers and software, but it's easier to manually change BIOS from the beginning.

QUICK Q&A

What happens if the CMOS battery runs out?
This dilemma is more commonly posed as a hypothesis than encountered as a reality. CMOS runs on very little power indeed and its battery should last for years and years. A good clue that the battery is failing is continually having to reset the date and time. The proper action is, of course, to replace the battery while the computer is turned off. Before starting, make a hand-written record of all the screens in the BIOS Setup program. You can then re-enter this information through BIOS when the new battery is installed.

Be sure to buy the right kind of battery for your motherboard: usually but not always 3V. It's also worth trying to install your new battery as quickly as you possibly can. The original CMOS record just might survive a second or two without power, in which case you can reboot and carry on exactly where you left off.

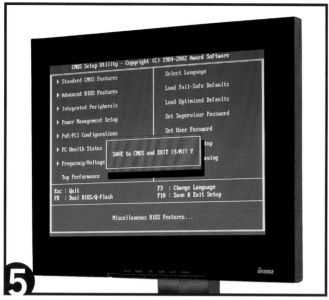

5 *When exiting the BIOS Setup program, it is important to save your changes to CMOS. Return to the main menu by pressing Escape. Press Escape again and then, when prompted, confirm that you want to save your changes by pressing Y. Alternatively, press F10 at any time to save your changes and exit BIOS in one move. Should you ever make a mistake or lose your place, simply type N when exiting and the CMOS record will not be altered or updated. If you forget to save your changes, you can always go back and do it all again.*

Just to recap, we have just set the date and time, disabled the motherboard's onboard audio chip in preparation for a sound card and ensured that the computer can boot from the CD drive.

BIOS updates

Motherboard manufacturers buy BIOS programs from a select few suppliers, including Phoenix Technologies (which now includes Award) and AMI. From time to time, such as when considering a processor upgrade or trying to enable support for a new technology without throwing out the motherboard, you may find it beneficial or even essential to upgrade the BIOS. No soldering iron is required; all BIOS chips these days are 'flash' upgradeable, which means you can download and install an update from the manufacturer's website. You certainly won't need a new BIOS when starting off with a new, recently made motherboard, however, and a non-essential BIOS update is not the best use of a slow Sunday afternoon (for which read: if it ain't broke, don't fix it).

Flash upgrade procedures vary but generally you download a couple of files from the internet, copy them to a floppy disk, enable the floppy disk drive as the first bootable device in your computer (back to BIOS again) and then run a Setup program that automatically installs the new BIOS.

The most important thing is to remember to make a copy of the CMOS record before starting out, just in case the upgrade fails halfway through and wipes the current settings. To do this, run the BIOS Setup program and copy down everything you see.

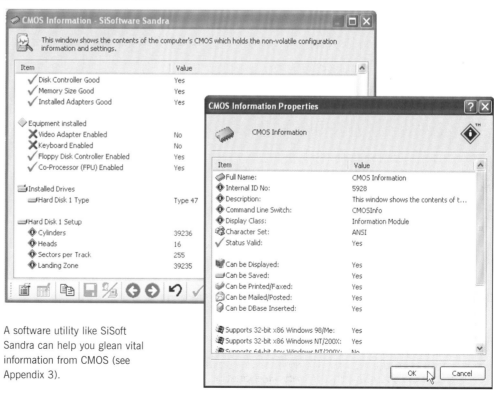

A software utility like SiSoft Sandra can help you glean vital information from CMOS (see Appendix 3).

PART 4 Installing Windows XP

With the CD drive enabled as a boot device, you can now install Windows straight from the installation CD without faffing around with floppies. We will describe the Windows XP Home Edition procedure here, but XP Professional installs in an almost identical manner.

As you probably know, Windows XP must be 'activated' with Microsoft to keep it working beyond an initial 30-day grace period. Because this procedure is sensitive to system changes – i.e. a major upgrade or component replacement can make XP demand re-activation – we would suggest that you postpone activation until you are happy with your overall hardware configuration.

Sit your computer upright on the table, connect a mouse and a keyboard, check that your monitor is plugged in and switched on, and press the on/off case switch to start the system. Now place the Windows XP CD in your CD-RW drive and turn the computer off and back on again. As it restarts, BIOS will launch the Windows Setup program.

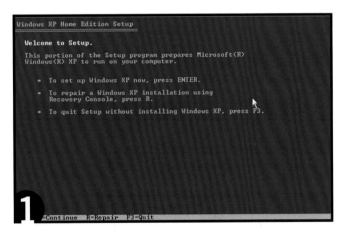

1 *Plain text on an all-blue background isn't particularly user-friendly, but all that follows is straightforward. Press Enter to kick-start Setup into action.*

2 *The licence agreement. This is not the place to argue the merits or otherwise of your very limited rights as laid down by Microsoft. Besides which, you have no choice. Press F8 to accept the terms of engagement.*

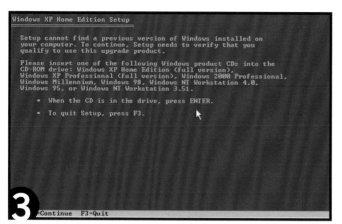

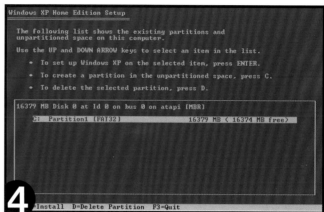

You'll only see this screen if you're using an 'Upgrade' rather than a 'Full' version of XP. Microsoft discounts new releases of Windows to previous customers but you must prove that you have at some point owned a qualifying version. Pop an original Windows 2000, Millennium Edition, 98, 95 or NT CD in the drive now and press Enter. Don't worry about having to remove the XP disc in the meantime – you'll be prompted to return it shortly.

Setup will now ask you where you wish to install Windows. Assuming that you have a new, clean, unpartitioned hard disk, the default suggestion C: is correct. You will also be asked which file system you wish to use. Windows XP is designed for NTFS rather than FAT, so select NTFS and let Setup format the disk accordingly.

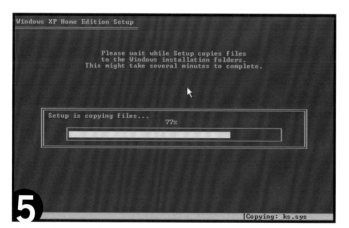

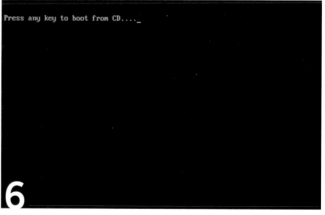

Setup will now ask you to replace the Windows XP CD in the drive, whereupon it copies the files it needs to the hard disk. Expect the system to reboot at the end of this process.

When your computer restarts, you will see a prompt inviting you to boot from the CD. However, this is rather misleading. Setup has already completed its first phase and can now boot straight from the hard disk. So do not press any keys, wait a minute and Setup will re-launch in a friendlier graphical guise.

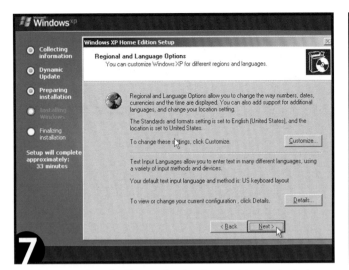

7 Windows now installs. Your active involvement is required at a few stages, beginning with the Regional and Language settings. Click the Customise button and tell Windows where you live.

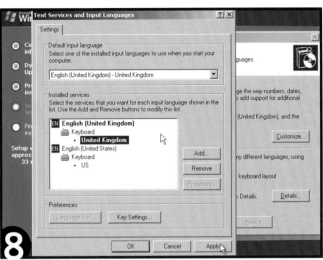

8 Next, click the Details button and change the input language and keyboard layout from US to UK (or whatever).

9 In the next screen, type in your name, or any other name you like, and optionally an organisation name.

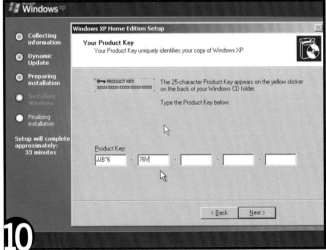

10 Now enter the Windows XP Product Key. If you get it wrong, which is easily done, Setup will refuse to continue until you get it right.

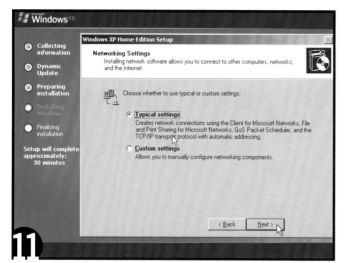

11 When prompted, give the computer its own name. This is essential for running a home network. In the next screen, accept the typical network settings.

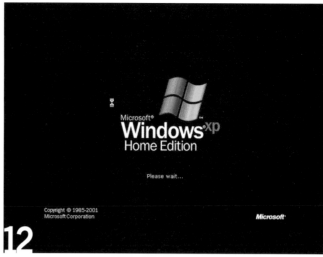

12 Setup now runs merrily on for a while and can be safely ignored. At the end of this process, it reboots your computer. Again, be sure not to boot from the CD; let Setup boot from the hard disk instead. Eventually, Windows itself makes an appearance. All that remains is to follow a few final setup steps.

Monitor driver

One of the first things Windows does is detect the presence of a monitor and load a default driver. It may also prompt you to install a driver supplied by the monitor manufacturer. You can do this now or later (check the manual for advice); what's important is that any Plug-and-Play monitor will work with Windows immediately.

Similarly, your AGP video card will function without any manual input, but it will not live up to its potential until you install a dedicated driver. Again, check the manual for guidance and pay occasional visits to the manufacturer's website. Driver updates are commonplace and usually improve performance, reliability or hardware compatibility in some way.

QUICK Q&A

Do I need Fdisk?
Fdisk is a DOS-based program that's useful for formatting and partitioning hard disk drives. You can use a floppy disk that contains Fdisk to ready your hard disk drive for an operating system but it's not necessary with later versions of Windows, including XP. So long as your CD drive is enabled as a bootable drive, the Windows Setup program will take care of everything.

QUICK Q&A

Can I run more than one operating system on my PC?
You certainly can. All you need are separate hard disk partitions with an operating system installed on each. The computer then treats these partitions as (almost) physically distinct drives, and with the aid of a boot manager program you can choose which operating system to load every time you restart.

However, if you envisage doing this, be sure to specify that Windows XP formats your bare drive with the FAT-32 file system during installation. A hard disk formatted with XP's preferred NTFS file system cannot be reverted to FAT-32, and most older versions of Windows (Windows 2000 excepted) will not run on an NTFS-formatted disk.

Alternatively, use an emulator like Virtual PC for Windows. This lets you run multiple operating systems from within Windows itself, which is really rather clever. Virtual PC used to be made by a company called Connectix but the technology has since been sold to Microsoft. The future of Virtual PC is now uncertain.

With Virtual PC you can run alternative operating systems within a window in Windows. It's a baby-plus-bathwater kind of thing.

PART 4 Installing the sound card

With the integrated audio chip disabled, you should have no trouble installing a sound card now. All recent sound cards use a PCI slot and your motherboard will have several. But which to use?

Well, the audio cables from your CD and DVD drives have to reach it, so look for the least awkward position that avoids audio cables being strung taut across the heatsink fan. Consider the position of any existing cards and look for pitfalls. If you cast your mind back to p.106, you'll remember that our AGP video card almost overhangs the neighbouring PCI slot. Rather than impeding the video card's fan, it would be better to leave a gap here and install the sound card in the next-but-one slot. Finally, check whether your sound card comes with an optional port bracket, and decide whether or not to use it. This sound card does, and we will, so the best solution is obviously to install the port bracket between the video card and the sound card.

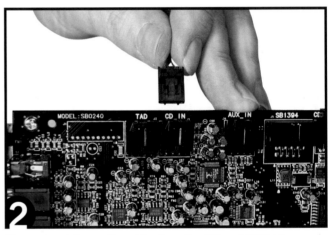

Turn off your computer, unplug it from the mains and take the usual antistatic precautions. Open the computer case and lay it on its side. Now familiarise yourself with the layout of the expansion card (i.e. read the manual), decide which PCI slot to use and remove the corresponding blanking plate from the case. Remove the card from its antistatic bag and carefully install it in the expansion slot. Be sure not to touch any components. Secure the card to the case chassis with the blanking plate screw.

Now connect the audio cables from the CD and DVD. The Audigy 2 Platinum card ships with an optional breakout box that sits in a 5.25-inch drive bay and provides an extra bunch of inputs and outputs, but we're not going to bother with that right now.

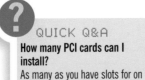

QUICK Q&A

How many PCI cards can I install?

As many as you have slots for on your motherboard. The PCI bus is natively 'Plug-and-Play', which means the computer can apportion system resources automatically and avoid hardware conflicts.

But we are going to connect the optional port bracket that supplies the computer with an alternative MIDI/games port. The original MIDI port, sited in the I/O panel, remains connected to the integrated audio chip but this has now been disabled.

Digital audio extraction

We mentioned earlier (p.102) that many drives support DAE. With speakers connected to the sound card, this is the time to find out.

First, establish that you can hear an audio CD when played in the CD drive. Then check that DAE has been enabled within Windows. In Windows XP, click Start, Control Panel, Performance & Maintenance and System. This launches the System Properties window. Look in the Hardware tab and click Device Manager. Here you will find a list of all the hardware devices in your computer. Click the little '+' sign next to DVD/CD-ROM drives and then double-click the drive in question. In the Properties tab, ensure that the 'Enable digital CD audio for this CD-ROM device' box is checked (ticked). If this option is greyed-out and unclickable, the drive does not support DAE and you'll definitely need to use an audio cable. Repeat with the DVD drive.

Now turn off your computer, remove the covers and disconnect the audio cable from either the drive or the sound card. Reboot and try playing the CD again. If you still hear sound, you know that the drive supports DAE and you can remove the cable altogether.

Remove the appropriate blanking plate and screw the port bracket into position in its place. Finally, replace the computer covers, plug it in and fire it up. Windows will identify the new component and ask for a driver. Pop the supplied CD-ROM in the drive and follow the directions. You should also install any applications software shipped with the card, and, of course, connect your speakers.

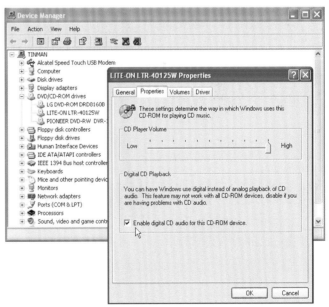

It's not such a huge deal, really, but Digital Audio Extraction lets you dispense with those fiddly internal sound cables. Anything that reduces the risk of cables snagging fans is welcome.

Loose ends

You should now have a fully-functioning, home-built, better-than-off-the-shelf PC at your disposal. Congratulations – the hard work is done! If everything is behaving as it should, now is the time to consider further hardware installations to complete the picture.

In a mid-tower case such as this it's not always easy to clear away extraneous clutter. Just ensure that cables are kept well away from fans and check that airflow in and out of the case is not blocked. Here, the sound card's bracket cable is rather too close to the video card's heatsink.

There is one final, rather pressing matter to take care of, namely tidying your PC's interior. The trouble here is that there's no 'right' way to do it as such; it's really just a matter of bunching together surplus power cables and tucking them out of the way … somewhere. A free drive bay is fine. Keep dangling cables away from fans and other components, and ensure that, so far as possible, cables do not impede airflow through the case. Your computer case manufacturer may have included a few plastic cable ties, or else you can use your own. Avoid metal ties, even if coated in paper or plastic, as these could short-circuit the motherboard. Again, the benefits of a tall tower case with plenty of room are apparent, but even a mid- or mini-tower can be kept reasonably tidy.

A full-tower case is a cinch to keep tidy. This example is further helped by the use of round IDE/ATA cables instead of the usual flat ribbon cables and a side-mounted hard disk drive.

Troubleshooting

Let's assume you've built your PC, turned it on for the first time … and nothing happens. You can't get into BIOS, let alone install Windows. How and where do you begin to troubleshoot?

In fact, identifying a problem at this stage is very much easier than down the road when you've got a printer, scanner, webcam and goodness knows what other hardware attached; not to mention 57 software programs doing their utmost to interfere with one another, a real risk of viruses and perhaps a utility suite that does more harm than good. Your computer will never be so easy to diagnose and cure as it is right now.

Check the cables

The very first step is all too obvious but all too often overlooked: check that all external cables are securely connected in the correct places:

☐	The computer's PSU should be plugged into a mains wall socket (or power gangplank).
☐	So should the monitor.
☐	The mains electricity supply should be turned on at the wall.
☐	The monitor should be connected to the video card's VGA or DVI output.
☐	The keyboard should be connected to the computer's PS/2-style keyboard port (not to a USB port, unless USB support has already been enabled in BIOS, and not to the mouse port).
☐	The PSU should be set to the correct voltage and turned on.

Now turn on the monitor. A power indication LED on the monitor housing should illuminate and, hopefully, you'll see something on the screen. If not, re-read the monitor manual and double-check that you've correctly identified the on/off switch and are not busy fiddling with the brightness or contrast controls. It's not always obvious which switch is which. If the power light still does not come on, it sounds like the monitor itself may be at fault. Try changing the fuse in the cable. Ideally, test the monitor with another PC.

Internal inspection

Now turn on the PC itself. Press the large on/off switch on the front of the case, not the smaller reset switch. You should hear the whirring of internal fans and either a single or a sequence of beeps. But let's assume that all seems lifeless. Again, check/change the fuse in the PSU power cable. If this doesn't help, unplug all cables, including the monitor, take off the case covers and lay the computer on its side. Now systematically check every internal connection. Again, here's a quick checklist to tick off:

- [ ] The PSU should be connected to the motherboard with a large 20-pin plug and also, if appropriate, with ATX 12V and ATX Auxiliary cables.

- [ ] The heatsink fan should be plugged into a power socket on the motherboard.

- [ ] The case fan(s) should be likewise connected.

- [ ] All drives should be connected to the appropriate sockets on the motherboard with ribbon cables.

- [ ] All drives should be connected to the PSU with power cables.

- [ ] The video card should be securely sited in its AGP slot.

- [ ] All other expansion cards should be likewise in place.

- [ ] Look for loose screws inside the case lest one should be causing a short-circuit.

- [ ] If your motherboard has jumpers, check that they are correctly set.

- [ ] Check the front panel connections. If the case's on/off switch is disconnected from the motherboard, you won't be able to start the system.

- [ ] Are any cables snagging on fans?

- [ ] Double-check that Pin 1 positions on cables and drives are correctly matched (confession time: we initially got this wrong with the unkeyed floppy cable plug).

- [ ] Are the retention clips on the memory DIMMs fully closed?

- [ ] Does anything on the motherboard look obviously broken or damaged?

Disconnect each cable in turn and look for bent pins on the plugs and sockets. These can usually be straightened with small, pointy pliers and a steady hand. Reconnect everything, including the monitor and power cable, and turn the computer on once more. Leave the covers off to aid observation. Does it now burst into life as if by magic? Rather gallingly, unplugging and replacing a cable is sometimes all it takes to fix an elusive but strictly temporary glitch.

PSU problems

Look for an LED on the motherboard (check the manual for its location). This should illuminate whenever the PSU is connected to the mains power and turned on, even when the computer itself is off. The LED confirms that the motherboard is receiving power; if it stays dark, the PSU itself may be at fault.

When you turn on the computer, do the fans remain static? Does the CD drive disc tray refuse to open? Is all depressingly dead? This would confirm it. Use an alternative power cable, perhaps borrowed from the monitor, just to be sure. If still nothing, remove and replace the PSU.

NEVER TRY TO OPEN OR REPAIR A PSU. Nor should you try running it while it's disconnected from the motherboard, as a PSU can only operate with a load.

Next steps

Let's assume that there is evidence of power flowing to the motherboard: the LED comes on and the heatsink and case fans spin. The PSU must be OK but there's still nothing on the monitor screen. Did you hear a beep as the computer powered up? This is a good thing. A sequence of beeps is generally a sign – a welcome sign, in fact – of specific, identifiable trouble. See the POST section below.

Check the keyboard. If anything is resting on the keys, remove it. This alone can cause a computer to pause. As the computer powers up, three lights on the keyboard should illuminate within the first few seconds. If they fail to do so, it's just possible that a dud keyboard is responsible for halting the entire system. Disconnect it and reboot the computer without a keyboard attached. If you now see a keyboard error message on the monitor screen where all was blank before, it looks like you need a new one. Connect an alternative keyboard to the computer and reboot again to confirm the diagnosis.

Another clue: if the computer partially boots but then stalls, check the memory count during the POST procedure (see below). If the RAM total differs from the memory you installed, it looks like you have a DIMM or RIMM problem to deal with. Remove, clean and replace each module. If that gets you nowhere, try booting with a single module in place, and experiment with each in turn. Check the motherboard manual for details here; a single module must usually be installed in a specific DIMM slot (usually DIMM1). If you can start the computer successfully at some point, you should be able to identify and exclude faulty modules. This isn't much help if you only have one module, of course. It's also much more complicated when working with Rambus modules that must be installed in pairs with Continuity RIMMs in spare RIMM slots.

Back to basics

Failing all of the above, disconnect all power and ribbon cables from the drives and the motherboard. Unplug and remove the video card and any other expansion cards, disconnect the case fan(s), and leave only a single memory module in place. In short, reduce the system to a bare-bones configuration where the only remaining connections are between the PSU and the motherboard: ATX power, ATX Auxiliary and ATX 12V. Do not remove the heatsink or processor, and leave all the front panel connections in place.

Now turn on the power once more. You should hear some diagnostic beeps from the BIOS. If so, see the POST section below and Appendix 2. If not, check the speaker connection.

If that doesn't resolve matters, turn off the computer, remove the power cable, and gradually, carefully, step-by-step, put it all back together again. Begin with the video card. Connect a monitor you know to be working and reboot the system. This will give you the added benefit of being able to read any onscreen error messages as you go along. If the screen stays blank, you know for sure that the video card is at fault. Replace it.

Reconnect a functioning keyboard next. Reboot, and check that your computer gets past POST – i.e. that you can successfully enter the BIOS Setup routine. Now reconnect the floppy drive ribbon and power cables and reboot once more. Reinstall the hard disk drive next, followed by the CD and DVD drives. Every step of the way, reboot the computer and ensure that it doesn't hang or abort during POST. At some point, the computer may refuse to start – and right there you will have identified your problem. Alternatively, it may start normally all the way through and you may never find out what the original stumbling block was. No matter: either way, you have successfully troubleshot your hardware hassles.

Power On Self Test (POST)

The very first thing a computer does when it starts is give itself a quick once-over to check that it still has a processor, memory and motherboard. If this Power On Self Test procedure finds a serious problem, or 'fatal error', it is likely to throw a wobbly and halt the computer in its tracks. That's the assumption we have been working on in this section.

However, it also gives you two useful diagnostic clues (actually three, but hexadecimal checkpoint codes are beyond the scope of this book).

First, assuming that the video card and monitor are both working, you should see some onscreen error messages. These may be self-explanatory or relatively obscure, depending on the problem and the BIOS manufacturer, but should offer at least some help. A memory error would indicate that one or more of your modules are either faulty or not properly installed; a 'hard disk not found' message would most likely point to a loose connection or perhaps a faulty IDE/ATA cable.

Secondly, so long as the case speaker is connected (see p.95), the motherboard will emit a series of POST-generated beeps. These can help you identify the specific component causing the problem.

We list some common beep code and error messages in Appendix 2 on p.132.

POST is a low-key but essential routine that the computer runs through before launching Windows. Keep an eye out for error messages on the screen and an ear out for beep codes.

5

PART 5

BUILD YORU OWN COMPUTER

Appendices

Appendix 1
Silence is golden ... well, copper and aluminium

If there is one thing the average desktop computer is not, it is quiet. Gallingly, the more high-powered you make it, the noisier it becomes. It all boils down to the cooling systems inside the case, i.e. a bunch of low-tech fans. There are fans in the PSU, fans built into the case, a fan on the processor heatsink, probably another on the North Bridge chip and yet another on the video card. Combined, they make a racket that's loud enough to be off-putting at best and to drown out music or game soundtracks at worst.

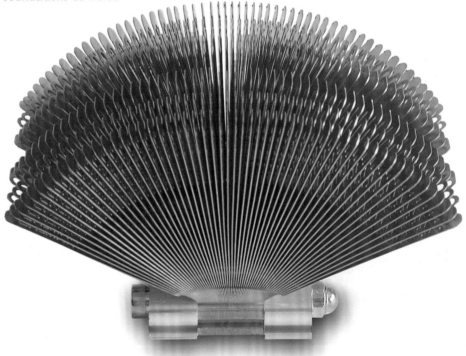

Freaky-looking it may be but this completely-silent Zalman 'Flower Cooler' can replace a boisterous CPU heatsink. All it needs is a really big, really quiet fan to supply it with fresh air.

However, there are some useful counter-measures available and here the DIY system builder can customise a computer to suit. For one, consider a passive heatsink for the processor, i.e. one without a powered fan. There are plenty of bizarre-looking but highly-effective heatsinks around that can keep the processor well within acceptable temperature limitations (under 75°Celsius for a Pentium 4).

Even chipset fans tend to be irritatingly intrusive, so you might care to remove the North Bridge heatsink and replace it with a silent fan-less alternative.

Most recent video cards also use fan-assisted heatsinks to cool the GPU. Here again it is often possible to replace the original with a silent version. Be careful, though: some of the latest video chips run so hot that a passive heatsink alone is not sufficient unless there is also a fan nearby to supply cool air.

There's little to do about a noisy PSU other than replace it with a quiet one – or, of course, to buy a quiet PSU in the first place. Check the specs and look for an acoustic noise level of about 30dB when the unit is running at 75% capacity.

Going further, you can even encase the hard disk drive in an acoustic enclosure and clad the interior of the case with sound-muffling panels.

Cooling caveats

Just a couple:

1. In smaller cases, the PSU is often located directly above the processor socket (as, in fact, in our project – see p.92). This generally rules out a passive heatsink because there simply isn't the necessary clearance over the processor. And even if you can squeeze one into the available space, don't forget that …

2. Even an elaborate super-effective passive heatsink needs some independent cooling. This is generally provided by a large, variable-speed ultra-quiet fan positioned directly above the heatsink and held in place with an angled bracket attached to the case. Again, this is not possible in most mid-tower cases.

In short, don't shell out for an inventive cooling solution unless you're sure your case can accommodate it. If you have an unobstructed view of the processor socket when the motherboard and PSU are both in place inside the case, you should be OK.

Consult Quiet PC for specialist advice and products, including the Zalman range of silent heatsinks (see Appendix 3).

If your chipset has a fan, consider replacing it with an efficient passive heatsink. So long as there is reasonable airflow inside the case, this will keep it cool and quiet.

If even the clicking of the hard disk drive drives you to distraction, encase your case in mufflers.

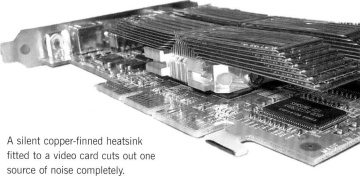

A silent copper-finned heatsink fitted to a video card cuts out one source of noise completely.

PART  # Appendix 2
Beep and error codes

As we discussed on p.93 and p.127, the motherboard –
or more precisely, the BIOS chip on the motherboard –
emits a sequence of beeps whenever it identifies a
problem that is serious enough to prevent the computer
from starting normally. If the BIOS does manage to get
the computer up and running, it can also generate
onscreen error messages that help you identify trouble
spots. Here we reprint the codes used by AMI and
Award, makers of two commonly used BIOS programs.

Phoenix, another major player, uses a rather more complicated
scheme that is beyond our scope here.

AMI BIOS beep codes

Number of Beeps	Problem	Action
1	Memory refresh timer error.	Remove each memory module, clean the connecting edge that plugs into the motherboard socket, and replace. If that doesn't work, try restarting with a single memory module and see if you can identify the culprit by a process of elimination. If you still get the error code, replace with known good modules.
2	Parity error.	As with 1 beep above.
3	Main memory read/write test error.	As with 1 beep above.
4	Motherboard timer not operational.	Either the motherboard is faulty or one of the expansion cards has a problem. Remove all cards except the video card and restart. If the motherboard still issues this beep code, it has a serious, probably fatal problem. If the beeps stop, replace the cards one at a time and restart each time. This should identify the guilty party.
5	Processor error.	As with 4 beeps above.
6	Keyboard controller BAT test error.	As with 4 beeps above.
7	General exception error.	As with 4 beeps above.
8	Display memory error.	The video card is missing, faulty or incorrectly installed. Remove, clean the connecting contacts and replace. If that doesn't work, try using a different video card. If you are using integrated video instead of a video card, the motherboard may be faulty.
9	ROM checksum error.	As with 4 beeps above.
10	CMOS shutdown register read/write error.	As with 4 beeps above.
11	Cache memory bad.	As with 4 beeps above.

AMIBIOS8 Checkpoint and Beep Code List version 1.2. Copyright of American Megatrends, Inc. Reprinted with permission.
All rights reserved.

AMI BIOS error codes Here are some examples of onscreen error messages:

Error	Action
Gate20 Error	The BIOS is unable to properly control the motherboard's Gate A20 function, which controls access of memory over 1MB. This may indicate a problem with the motherboard.
Multi-Bit ECC Error	This message will only occur on systems using ECC-enabled memory modules. ECC memory has the ability to correct single-bit errors that may occur from faulty memory modules. A multiple bit corruption of memory has occurred, and the ECC memory algorithm cannot correct it. This may indicate a defective memory module.
Parity Error	Fatal Memory Parity Error. System halts after displaying this message.
Boot Failure	This is a generic message indicating the BIOS could not boot from a particular device. This message is usually followed by other information concerning the device.
Invalid Boot Diskette	A diskette was found in the drive, but it is not configured as a bootable diskette.
Drive Not Ready	The BIOS was unable to access the drive because it indicated it was not ready for data transfer. This is often reported by drives when no media is present.
A: Drive Error	The BIOS attempted to configure the A: drive during POST, but was unable to properly configure the device. This may be because of a bad cable or faulty diskette drive.
Insert BOOT diskette in A:	The BIOS attempted to boot from the A: drive, but could not find a proper boot diskette.
Reboot and Select proper Boot device or Insert Boot Media in selected Boot device	BIOS could not find a bootable device in the system and/or removable media drive does not contain media.
NO ROM BASIC	This message occurs on some systems when no bootable device can be detected.
Primary Master Hard Disk Error	The IDE/ATAPI device configured as Primary Master could not be properly initialized by the BIOS. This message is typically displayed when the BIOS is trying to detect and configure IDE/ATAPI devices in POST.
Primary Slave Hard Disk Error	The IDE/ATAPI device configured as Primary Slave could not be properly initialized by the BIOS. This message is typically displayed when the BIOS is trying to detect and configure IDE/ATAPI devices in POST.
Secondary Master Hard Disk Error	The IDE/ATAPI device configured as Secondary Master could not be properly initialized by the BIOS. This message is typically displayed when the BIOS is trying to detect and configure IDE/ATAPI devices in POST.
Secondary Slave Hard Disk Error	The IDE/ATAPI device configured as Secondary Slave could not be properly initialized by the BIOS. This message is typically displayed when the BIOS is trying to detect and configure IDE/ATAPI devices in POST.

AMI BIOS error codes continued:

Error	Action
Primary Master Drive – ATAPI Incompatible	The IDE/ATAPI device configured as Primary Master failed an ATAPI compatibility test. This message is typically displayed when the BIOS is trying to detect and configure IDE/ATAPI devices in POST.
Primary Slave Drive – ATAPI Incompatible	The IDE/ATAPI device configured as Primary Slave failed an ATAPI compatibility test. This message is typically displayed when the BIOS is trying to detect and configure IDE/ATAPI devices in POST.
Secondary Master Drive – ATAPI Incompatible	The IDE/ATAPI device configured as Secondary Master failed an ATAPI compatibility test. This message is typically displayed when the BIOS is trying to detect and configure IDE/ATAPI devices in POST.
Secondary Slave Drive – ATAPI Incompatible	The IDE/ATAPI device configured as Secondary Slave failed an ATAPI compatibility test. This message is typically displayed when the BIOS is trying to detect and configure IDE/ATAPI devices in POST.
S.M.A.R.T. Capable but Command Failed	The BIOS tried to send a S.M.A.R.T. message to a hard disk, but the command transaction failed. This message can be reported by an ATAPI device using the S.M.A.R.T. error reporting standard. S.M.A.R.T. failure messages may indicate the need to replace the hard disk.
S.M.A.R.T. Command Failed	The BIOS tried to send a S.M.A.R.T. message to a hard disk, but the command transaction failed. This message can be reported by an ATAPI device using the S.M.A.R.T. error reporting standard. S.M.A.R.T. failure messages may indicate the need to replace the hard disk.
S.M.A.R.T. Status BAD, Backup and Replace	A S.M.A.R.T. capable hard disk sends this message when it detects an imminent failure. This message can be reported by an ATAPI device using the S.M.A.R.T. error reporting standard. S.M.A.R.T. failure messages may indicate the need to replace the hard disk.
S.M.A.R.T. Capable and Status BAD	A S.M.A.R.T. capable hard disk sends this message when it detects an imminent failure. This message can be reported by an ATAPI device using the S.M.A.R.T. error reporting standard. S.M.A.R.T. failure messages may indicate the need to replace the hard disk.
BootSector Write!!	The BIOS has detected software attempting to write to a drive's boot sector. This is flagged as possible virus activity. This message will only be displayed if Virus Detection is enabled in AMIBIOS Setup.
VIRUS: Continue (Y/N)?	If the BIOS detects possible virus activity, it will prompt the user. This message will only be displayed if Virus Detection is enabled in AMIBIOS Setup.
DMA-2 Error	Error initializing secondary DMA controller. This is a fatal error, often indicating a problem with system hardware.
DMA Controller Error	POST error while trying to initialize the DMA controller. This is a fatal error, often indicating a problem with system hardware.

AMI BIOS error codes continued:

Error	Action
CMOS Date/Time Not Set	The CMOS Date and/or Time are invalid. This error can be resolved by readjusting the system time in AMIBIOS Setup.
CMOS Battery Low	CMOS Battery is low. This message usually indicates that the CMOS battery needs to be replaced. It could also appear when the user intentionally discharges the CMOS battery.
CMOS Settings Wrong	CMOS settings are invalid. This error can be resolved by using AMIBIOS Setup.
CMOS Checksum Bad	CMOS contents failed the Checksum check. Indicates that the CMOS data has been changed by a program other than the BIOS or that the CMOS is not retaining its data due to malfunction. This error can typically be resolved by using AMIBIOS Setup.
Keyboard Error	Keyboard is not present or the hardware is not responding when the keyboard controller is initialized.
Keyboard/Interface Error	Keyboard Controller failure. This may indicate a problem with system hardware.
System Halted	The system has been halted. A reset or power cycle is required to reboot the machine. This message appears after a fatal error has been detected.

Award BIOS beep codes

Number of Beeps	Problem	Action
1 long beep followed by 2 short beeps	Video card problem	Remove the card, clean the connecting edge that plugs into the motherboard socket, and replace. If that doesn't work, try an alternative video card to establish whether the problem lies with the card or the AGP slot. If you are using integrated video instead of a video card, the motherboard may be faulty.
Any other beeps	Memory problem	Remove each memory module, clean the connecting edge that plugs into the motherboard socket, and replace. If that doesn't work, try restarting with a single memory module and see if you can identify the culprit by a process of elimination. If you still get the error code, replace with known good modules

Award BIOS error codes Here are the standard Award onscreen error messages:

Error	Action
BIOS ROM checksum error – System halted	The checksum of the BIOS code in the BIOS chip is incorrect, indicating the BIOS code may have become corrupt. Contact your system dealer to replace the BIOS.
CMOS battery failed	The CMOS battery is no longer functional. Contact your system dealer for a replacement battery.
CMOS checksum error – Defaults loaded	Checksum of CMOS is incorrect, so the system loads the default equipment configuration. A checksum error may indicate that CMOS has become corrupt. This error may have been caused by a weak battery. Check the battery and replace if necessary.
CPU at nnnn	Displays the running speed of the CPU.
Display switch is set incorrectly	The display switch on the motherboard can be set to either monochrome or colour. This message indicates the switch is set to a different setting from that indicated in Setup. Determine which setting is correct, and then either turn off the system and change the jumper, or enter Setup and change the VIDEO selection.
Press ESC to skip memory test	The user may press Esc to skip the full memory test.
Floppy disk(s) fail	Cannot find or initialize the floppy drive controller or the drive. Make sure the controller is installed correctly. If no floppy drives are installed, be sure the Diskette Drive selection in Setup is set to NONE or AUTO.
HARD DISK initializing. Please wait a moment.	Some hard drives require extra time to initialize.
HARD DISK INSTALL FAILURE	Cannot find or initialize the hard drive controller or the drive. Make sure the controller is installed correctly. If no hard drives are installed, be sure the Hard Drive selection in Setup is set to NONE.
Hard disk(s) diagnosis fail	The system may run specific disk diagnostic routines. This message appears if one or more hard disks return an error when the diagnostics run.
Keyboard error or no keyboard present	Cannot initialize the keyboard. Make sure the keyboard is attached correctly and no keys are pressed during POST. To purposely configure the system without a keyboard, set the error halt condition in Setup to HALT ON ALL, BUT KEYBOARD. The BIOS then ignores the missing keyboard during POST.
Keyboard is locked out – Unlock the key	This message usually indicates that one or more keys have been pressed during the keyboard tests. Be sure no objects are resting on the keyboard.
Memory Test	This message displays during a full memory test, counting down the memory areas being tested.
Memory test fail	If POST detects an error during memory testing, additional information appears giving specifics about the type and location of the memory error.
Override enabled - Defaults loaded	If the system cannot boot using the current CMOS configuration, the BIOS can override the current configuration with a set of BIOS defaults designed for the most stable, minimal-performance system operations.
Press TAB to show POST screen	System OEMs may replace the Phoenix Technologies' AwardBIOS POST display with their own proprietary display. Including this message in the OEM display permits the operator to switch between the OEM display and the default POST display.
Primary master hard disk fail	POST detects an error in the primary master IDE hard drive.
Primary slave hard disk fail	POST detects an error in the secondary master IDE hard drive.
Secondary master hard disk fail	POST detects an error in the primary slave IDE hard drive.
Secondary slave hard disk fail	POST detects an error in the secondary slave IDE hard drive.

Appendix 3
Further resources

Here are some useful links that will lead you to more detailed information on selected subjects:

High Street retailers

Maplin	www.maplin.co.uk
PC World	www.pcworld.co.uk

Web/mail order retailers

Dabs	www.dabs.com
Bosse Computers	www.bossecomputers.com
Tekheads	www.tekheads.co.uk
Overclockers	www.overclockers.co.uk
Quiet PC	www.quietpc.com/uk

Computer fair contacts

Computer Fairs Information	www.computerfairs.co.uk
Northern Computer Markets	www.computermarkets.co.uk
Computer Markets Online	www.computermarketsonline.co.uk
The Show Guide	www.theshowguide.co.uk
All-Formats Computer Fairs	www.afm96.co.uk
The Best Event	www.bestevent.co.uk
Abacus Computer Fairs	www.fairs.co.uk

B-Grade retailers

Morgan Computers	www.morgancomputers.co.uk
Dabs	www.dabs.com

High street and web retailers also sell-off B-Grade stock from time to time; look for bargain bins, manager's specials and the like.

Consumer rights information

Trading Standards Institute	www.tradingstandards.gov.uk
Office of Fair Trading	www.oft.gov.uk

Processor manufacturers

Intel	www.intel.com
AMD	www.amd.com

Chipset information

Intel	www.intel.com
AMD	www.amd.com
ALi	www.ali.com.tw
VIA	www.via.com.tw
SiS	www.sis.com
Nvidia	www.nvidia.com

Intel and AMD also publish lists of motherboards that are compatible with their processors:

Intel	http://indigo.intel.com/mbsg/
AMD	http://www.amd.com/us-en/Processors/TechnicalResources/0,,30_182_869_4348^7923,00.html

(or http://makeashorterlink.com/?J3FA56FB3)

Memory information

Crucial Technology	http://support.crucial.com
Kingston Technology	www.kingston.com/tools/umg/default.asp
Rambus	www.rambus.com

Memory tools

Crucial Technology	www.crucial.com/uk
Kingston Technology	www.kingston.com/ukroot

Utilities

Intel Chipset Identification Utility
www.intel.com/support/chipsets/inf/chipsetid.htm

Sandra	www.sisoftware.co.uk
Ontrack JumperViewer	www.ontrack.com/jumperviewer

Audio technology

Dolby Labs	www.dolby.com
DTS	www.dtsonline.com
Steinberg	www.steinberg.net
THX	www.thx.com
DirectX	www.microsoft.com/windows/directx

Graphics technology

Nvidia	www.nvidia.com
ATI	www.ati.com
Matrox	www.matrox.com

CD/DVD technology

CD-Recordable FAQ	www.cdrfaq.org
DVD Demystified	www.dvddemystified.com
DVD+RW Alliance	www.dvdrw.com
DVD Forum	www.dvdforum.org
Optical Storage Technology Association (for MultiRead)	www.osta.org

Hardware review sites

Tom's Hardware Guide	www.tomshardware.com
Motherboards.org	www.motherboards.org
ExtremeTech	www.extremetech.com
Active Hardware	www.active-hardware.com
Anand Tech	www.anandtech.com
Digital-Daily	www.digital-daily.com

BIOS updates and information

Phoenix	www.phoenix.com
Award	www.unicore.com
AMI	www.megatrends.com
Bios-Drivers	www.bios-drivers.com

Manufacturers featured

Gigabyte	http://uk.giga-byte.com
Creative Labs	www.europe.creative.com
Plextor	www.plextor.be
LG Electronics	www.lge.com
Belkin	www.belkin.co.uk
Zalman	www.zalmanusa.com
Iiyama	www.iiyama.co.uk
Lian Li/Enermax	www.bossecomputers.com

Software featured

Windows XP	www.microsoft.com
Virtual PC	www.microsoft.com/windowsxp/virtualpc

All you ever wanted to know about ...

Form factors	www.formfactors.org
Serial ATA	www.serialata.org
Wireless networking	www.wi-fi.org

PART **5**

Appendix 4
Abbreviations & acronyms

2D/3D	Two-dimensional/three-dimensional
2x/4x, etc.	Double-speed/quadruple-speed, etc.
A3D	Aureal 3D
AC '97	Audio Codec '97
AGP	Accelerate Graphics Port
AMR	Audio Modem Riser
ASIO	Audio Stream In/Out
ATA	Advanced Technology Attachment
ATAPI	Advanced Technology Attachment Packet Interface
ATX	Advanced Technology Extended
BIOS	Basic In/Out System
CD	Compact Disc
CD-DA	Compact Disc – Digital Audio
CD-R	Compact Disc – Recordable
CD-ROM	Compact Disc – Read-Only Memory
CD-RW	Compact Disc – Rewriteable
CMOS	Complementary Metal-Oxide Semiconductor
CNR	Communications and Networking Riser
CPU	Central Processing Unit
CRIMM	Continuity Rambus Inline Memory Module
DAE	Digital Audio Extraction
dB	Decibel
DDR-RAM	Double Data Rate Random-Access Memory
DIMM	Dual Inline Memory Module
DMA	Direct Memory Access
DSL	Digital Subscriber Line
DTS	Digital Theater Systems
DVD	Digital Versatile Disc
DVD-RAM	Digital Versatile Disc – Random-Access Memory
DVD-ROM	Digital Versatile Disc – Read-Only Memory
DVD-R/RW	Digital Versatile Disc – Recordable/Rewriteable
DVD+R/RW	Digital Versatile Disc – Recordable/Rewriteable
DVI	Digital Visual Interface
EAX	Environmental Audio Extensions
FAQ	Frequently Asked Questions
FAT	File Allocation Table
FSB	Front-Side Bus
GB	Gigabyte
GPU	Graphics Processing Unit
HDD	Hard Disk Drive
HT	Hyper-Threading
I/O	Input/Output
ICH	Integrated Controller Hub
IDE	Integrated Drive Electronics
IEC	International Electrotechnical Commission
IEEE	Institute of Electrical and Electronic Engineers
ISA	Industry Standard Architecture
KB	Kilobyte
KHz	Kilohertz
LAN	Local Area Network
LED	Light-Emitting Diode
MB	Megabyte
Mbps	Megabits-per-second
MCH	Memory Controller Hub
MHz	Megahertz
MIDI	Musical Instrument Digital Interface
MP3	Motion Picture Experts Group Audio Layer Three
MPEG	Motion Picture Experts Group
NIC	Network Interface Card
NTFS	New Technology File System
P4	Pentium 4
PC	Personal Computer
PCI	Peripheral Component Interconnect
PDA	Personal Digital Assistant
PDF	Portable Document Format
PnP	Plug-and-Play
POST	Power On Self Test
PS/2	Personal System/2
PSU	Power Supply Unit
RAID	Redundant Array of Independent Disks
RAM	Random-Access Memory
RIMM	Rambus Inline Memory Module
S.M.A.R.T.	Self-Monitoring Analysis and Reporting Technology
SATA	Serial Advanced Technology Attachment
SCSI	Small Computer Systems Interface
SD-RAM	Synchronous Dynamic Random-Access Memory
SPDIF	Sony/Philips Digital Interface
TFT	Thin Film Transistor
THX	Tomlinson Holman Experiment
UPS	Uninterruptible Power Supply
USB	Universal Serial Port
VGA	Video Graphics Array
Wi-Fi	Wireless Fidelity
ZIF	Zero Insertion Force

Index

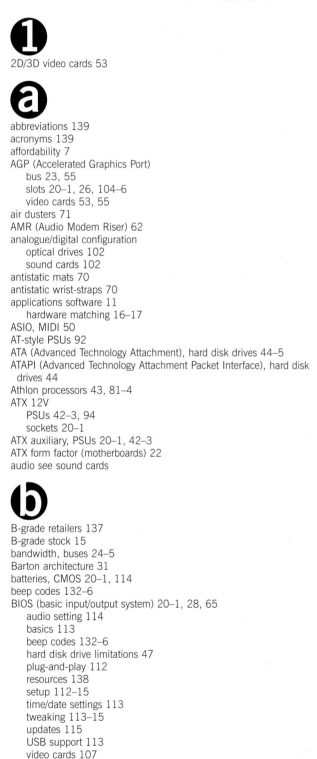

1

2D/3D video cards 53

ACKNOWLEDGEMENTS

The author and publisher would like to thank the following companies for their help in the preparation of this manual:

AMI	Iiyama
Blitz PR	Kingston Technology
Bosse Computers	LaCie
Catalysis Communications	LG Electronics
CIT PR	Maplin Electronics
Crucial Technology	Noiseworks
Dixons	Phoenix Technologies
Fresh Communications	Prodigy Communications
Gigabyte Technology	Quiet PC
Hotwire PR	

Author	**Kyle MacRae**
Copy Editor	**John Hardaker**
Photography	**Iain McLean**
Front cover illustration	**Digital Progression**
Design	**Simon Larkin**
Page build	**James Robertson**
Index	**Nigel d'Auvergne**
Project Manager	**Louise McIntyre**